PORTRAITS OF CHICAGO

SIDEWALKS

RICK KOGAN

PHOTOGRAPHS BY CHARLES OSGOOD

NORTHWESTERN UNIVERSITY PRESS

EVANSTON, ILLINOIS

Northwestern University Press
www.nupress.northwestern.edu

Printed in China

10   9   8   7   6   5   4   3   2   1

ISBN 0-8101-2349-5

Page vi (left): Sunrise over Chicago
Page vi (right): Jockey at Hawthorne Race Course
Pages vi–vii: Wall mural in Pilsen
Page vii (left): Sherman Park
Page vii (right): Sunrise on Promontory Point
Page viii: Montgomery Ward building and the John Hancock Center
Page x: Two sidewalks in Old Edgebrook
Page 242: Cloud Gate at Millennium Park
Page 246: Dirksen Federal Building plaza

Library of Congress Cataloging-in-Publication data are available from the
Library of Congress.

This book is printed on acid-free paper.

Book design by Kim Bartko

CONTENTS

PREFACE

Sidewalks was born eight years ago when I felt the need to get out of the office and remind myself what it was like to be a newspaper reporter after too many years (only two, actually, but that was two too many) as an editor.

I approached photographer Charles Osgood with the idea.

"I'll grab a notebook and a pen," I said. "You grab some cameras and let's go."

"Where?" he asked.

"Anywhere," I said.

"Okay," he said. "Let's go."

We've been on the road ever since, hitting hundreds of corners in this remarkable city and areas beyond, randomly exploring and coming into contact with people and places and things that quietly share and shape our place on the planet. You will meet some of them in this book, 113 of them to be exact, out of the nearly four hundred (and counting) columns we have produced.

The mix is an eclectic one. You will visit a two-story outhouse and an urban garden named for a junkie, meet a man who builds large things with toothpicks and a woman who loves accordions. Osgood likes to eat, and so you will find a number of interesting places that serve food—and a few that pour a decent cocktail, one of my favorite things. Many of the *Sidewalks* subjects have to do with art and that is because much of our careers has been spent writing about and photographing artistic endeavors, and it seems to us that art—whether in the form of a mural or a majestic building—enriches the environment more profoundly than does another expressway-paving project.

Most of the characters or sites or items in this book could not (nor do they even deserve to) make front-page news. They are what are called ordinary people and simple things, but there is truth in their stories and sometimes even beauty.

Though you could surely use this book as an enjoyable if unconventional guide, be aware that some of our subjects are no longer around—dead, razed, shuttered. I have chosen not to update any of the entries; the dates you will see on the pages are the dates the stories ran in the *Chicago Tribune Magazine*. You should be allowed to discover things as we did, feel the same exciting jolt when listening to the stories, even if some are now only echoes.

SIDEWALKS

MORNING ON MAXWELL

IT IS A SUN-SPLASHED MORNING in autumn and Maxwell Street is a forlorn place. The curbs are broken, the sidewalks smashed and thrown askew as if by a small earthquake. It's a shattered, tattered, and shuttered street. The block east of Halsted Street is a mess of iron grates, plywood, and broken glass windows, barely able to echo the vibrancy that was here for more than a century, a disorderly but delightfully dizzying mix of immigrant cultures and commerce.

The city shut down the Maxwell Street market in 1994, and now there is an empty lot on the north side of the street, covered with wood chips, and next to it a makeshift shrine. A sculpture spells MAX in ten-foot-tall letters made of railroad ties, and near it is the *Maxwell Street Wall of Fame,* a mural filled with names of former area residents such as bluesman Bo Diddley, jazzman Benny Goodman, and former Supreme Court justice Arthur Goldberg.

Near the mural is posted a large cardboard petition, the work of a ragtag group of activists, citizens, and blues performers called the Maxwell Street Historic Preservation Coalition. It is intended for David Broski, chancellor of the University of Illinois at Chicago, which plans further expansion into the area. Only five names and addresses are scrawled on the petition.

Too bad. Though the coalition is bound to lose its fight with progress, are there not ways to save a slice of Maxwell Street, to memorialize its significance, its soul?

On the corner, bluesman Bobby Davis plays and Jim's Original ("Since 1939") is selling Polish sausages and other sandwiches, all with "free fries." On a crumbling curb across the street, a fifty-two-year-old man named Reginald Brown sits with a bag of his belongings.

A stranger strikes up a conversation that will last a few minutes. But it is the initial exchange that captures the state of the street.

"What's going on?" Brown is asked.

"Nothing," he says.

NOVEMBER 1, 1998

A LIFE ON THE WATER

OF ALL THE GREGARIOUS CHARACTERS who frequent Wise Guy's Corner at the bar in the Billy Goat Tavern, none looks healthier or happier than Bob Borgstrom. It has a lot to do with the way he spends his days, as owner and one of the captains of the Wendella Boats on the Chicago River under the north end of the Michigan Avenue Bridge.

Borgstrom is almost seventy now and began working at fourteen for his father, Albert Borgstrom, who started out in 1935 operating a ninety-seven-passenger wooden boat from Navy Pier out onto the lake. He and his boat moved to the river in 1938 and, except during World War II, successfully operated sightseeing tours of "the world's most beautiful skyline." In 1962, at the urging of Ben Heineman, then chairman of the Chicago and North Western Railway, Wendella inaugurated boat commuter service between the train stations near Madison Street and the Michigan Avenue Bridge.

Now, during morning and evening rush hours, Wendella boats transport hundreds of commuters, such as one lawyer who says, "There is serenity on the water. This takes the edge off work."

Bob Borgstrom knows the river as well as anyone has ever known it and says that "forty years ago it was an ugly, filthy river, and twenty years ago it wasn't much better. But the mayor's done a great job getting the river clean and allowing the banks to come alive with trees, small parks, and restaurants. That's helped me appreciate it more. And the wildlife is amazing—geese, ducks. I haven't been able to put some flowers where I want to on our dock because there's a duck nesting there."

Wendella is a family business. Among the firm's thirty-some employees is Bob's wife, Lila. He met her at a party at Foster Avenue Beach when he was a student at Senn High School. The couple's sons, Steven and Michael, also work for the company. Four granddaughters are not unfamiliar with the boats and the water.

When he takes a vacation, Borgstrom goes fishing in the Florida Keys. When he stops into the Billy Goat sometimes after work, he will—perhaps because he looks so tan and lively—attract the attention of a stranger who will ask, "Who's that guy with the white hair?"

Someone in the know will say, "That's Bob. He's the guy who runs the boats."

Invariably and understandably, that stranger will get an envious look on his or her face.

JUNE 6, 1999

THE FLOCK OF FIFTY-THIRD

THE WORLD GYM IN HYDE PARK has a wall of windows facing East Fifty-third Street, and one rainy afternoon the club's manager, Clarence Hawkins, watches a group of six strangely attired teenagers purposefully marching west. In many parts of the city, this is an alarming sight, playing into the prejudices and harsh realities that shadow the lives of black teens. For a moment Hawkins, a former competitive power lifter and bodybuilder, looks worried.

"Trouble? It looks okay, I guess," he says.

There is a subtle but crucial difference between trouble and mischief, and these neighborhood kids, fourteen and fifteen years old, are safely, if seriously, on mischief's side. They are dressed in plastic garbage bags, parts of grocery boxes, bandannas, leaves, and small branches. And they are on their way to Boston Market, a few steps west, where they plan to stage a protest. They are a loquacious bunch, bright and personable. One of them is particularly playful: "This is a government conspiracy. They put the wrong serum in my bloodstream and messed up my mind."

The others laugh, standing on the rain-slicked sidewalk in front of Boston Market. The sign they have made is a soggy and incomprehensible mess, but their message is clear: they want better food and lower prices. The neighborhood is getting too "stuck up." They want to be treated respectfully, even if they are kids.

These teens have staged similar protests this summer in front of the nearby Sony Theaters and Video Connection store. There has been no trouble. They are viewed as cutups rather than agitators.

"We are not trying to change the whole world," says one. "Just our part of it."

Back at the World Gym, Hawkins nods his head at hearing what the teens are doing. Hawkins lives on the Southwest Side but likes working in Hyde Park.

"There's a very interesting mix of people down here," he says, smiling. "So they're protesters, huh? I have a ten-year-old son, and the most important thing is for him to get a good education. Then he can be anything he wants to be."

By now the protesters have moved on. They call themselves the Flock, as in "Birds of a feather . . ." Before that they were the Heart Association, as in "That's what you gotta have—heart."

SEPTEMBER 13, 1998

A GOOD WALK UNSPOILED

ZETA MOORE OF HIGHLAND PARK, nine years old and full of fine stories, was telling me the other day that one of her prized possessions is a golden coin that she recently won "playing golf."

She didn't have to tell me where she won this rare item; I'm pretty sure my brother still has similar coins that he won more than thirty-five years ago. It had to be Par-King, that magical miniature golf course on Dempster Street in Morton Grove. When told of this, Zeta said, "Maybe I will keep mine, too," and I thought how wonderful it is that there remain a certain, if decreasing, number of experiences that can bind generations.

The last time I visited Par-King (there is a newer course at 21711 North Milwaukee Avenue in Lincolnshire, but I am partial to the original) was in July. It is harder to remember the first time. It must have been shortly after it was built in 1961, for the surrounding land was mostly farms and the trip from the city, my father behind the wheel, was long enough to seem like a vacation.

It was created by three sons of George Boznos, who long ago farmed the land and operated a grocery store there. Nick, Gus, and Sam Boznos built a whimsical, patriotic course. There is a replica of the Prudential Building (the tallest structure in Chicago when the course was built; the Lincolnshire course features the Sears Tower), which asks you to putt into a moving elevator. There is a red roller coaster, a Mount Rushmore, a Statue of Liberty, a castle, an alligator, a clown. And, of course, there is the eighteenth hole, the source of the golden coins if your ball drops into the correct slot.

Playing the course is a blast, still. And, truth be told, miniature golf is a much more satisfying and sensible pursuit than the real thing. It does not offer much in the way of humiliation. It takes but modest athletic ability. It is virtually impossible to lose your ball. And it is possible for a round to end with a happy golden coin shout rather than just a long sigh of relief.

AUGUST 26, 2001

HIGH ON RELIGION

OSGOOD AND I HAVE HAD PEOPLE tell us that they feel close to God on a bar stool, in the bleachers at Wrigley Field, or staring at the lake. We listen to them. We don't argue. But if there is a God in heaven and heaven's in the sky, then it might be argued that there is no person closer to God than Dr. Philip L. Blackwell, senior pastor of First United Methodist Church at the Chicago Temple.

The church crowns the building at the southeast corner of Clark and Washington Streets, a spot notable because it is the site of the oldest congregation in the city. It dates to 1838, when a log church was moved there from across the river, where the congregation began in 1831.

The structure now on the corner was built in 1924. Designed by the firm of Holabird and Roche, it was for years the tallest building in the city, stretching 568 feet to the top of its spire. Its first four floors are devoted to church operations, while offices occupy floors 5 to 21, many of them filled with lawyers (Clarence Darrow once worked on the sixth floor). Above that is the church: the sanctuary, able to seat a thousand people; the Dixon Chapel and James Parlor, used for such events as Sunday school, weddings, and baptisms; and the remarkable Sky Chapel, as beautiful a room as there is in this area, created in 1952 by a donation from Myrtle Walgreen in memory of her late husband, Charles, who founded the drugstore chain.

A native of downstate Danville, the sixty-year-old Blackwell came to the Chicago Temple in 2001 after serving in administrative roles and, for more than a decade, as the senior minister at Trinity United Methodist Church in Wilmette. He is funny, and he's smart, and he cares passionately about the city. He has degrees from the University of Wisconsin, Yale, and the University of Chicago. He lives in the building in which he works, and so his commute is "oh, twenty-two seconds, give or take." His congregation numbers a thousand and, he says proudly, "they come from every city zip code and dozens in the suburbs. We are a diverse group, and I am grittily determined to be urban. We are defined by our location. I think we are progressive, which is a nice word for liberal. We are only one voice in the city, but I want to have discussions here that aren't taking place at City Hall."

He writes a column for the church publication, *Carillon,* where he tackles such dicey subjects as war and gay marriage. It's encouraging that a man who lives in the clouds can so passionately relate to those on the ground.

AUGUST 15, 2004

RUNNING THE TABLES

I COULD TELL YOU NOW about the afternoon I spent playing pool with Vanna White, who has her own cue, but it was too humiliating. Otherwise, I have wonderful pool memories going all the way back to subterranean Bensinger's, on Broadway near Diversey Parkway, and progressing through the years (and a haze of smoke) to such places as the Golden Eight Ball on Walton Street and dozens of others, most of them now gone.

Pool halls—or billiard parlors, to those with delicate sensibilities—have been a part of the urban sports landscape since the mid–eighteenth century, growing so popular that by the 1920s there were more than forty-two thousand pool halls in the country. Many were massive rooms, such as Detroit's Recreation, with 142 tables, and Chicago's W. P. Mussey in the Loop, with 88.

Popularity declined until the 1961 movie *The Hustler* created a boom. But most of the new pool halls built at that time were called family billiard centers, and though families may have sampled them, they didn't stay.

The last pool boom came in the late 1980s and early 1990s, when it seemed as if billiard palaces were springing up as fast as Starbucks do today. Such chic parlors/clubs as Muddler's on Clybourn and Lucky's on Institute Place were the direct result of the success of the 1986 movie *The Color of Money,* known as *The Hustler II.*

But that fad, too, faded. Though there are still quite a few places to play pool (even in restaurants), to find the serious players and the proper ambience one must travel to the neighborhoods, to such spots as Marie's Golden Cue, at 3241 West Montrose Avenue, where Osgood captured Marco Pugo shooting while brothers Pablo and Johnny observed.

This is a venerable twenty-table place that was going to be used as one of the locations for *The Color of Money* until the owners made it look too clean. Local scenes were filmed at Chris's Billiards, at 4637 North Milwaukee Avenue.

That should tell you something. The image of pool has always been and remains scruffy. That's a shame. Chicago playwright David Mamet, who spent time at Bensinger's in his youth, once wrote an essay in which he praised pool halls as wonderful places to be alone. He's got a point, but such places have always been for me lively and companionable arenas of sharp sounds and bright colors and colorful characters, all of them trying to play the angles.

APRIL 28, 2002

EVEN IN THE CRIME-RIDDEN TIMES in which we live, it is easier than you might ever have imagined to find criminals and the evidence of their misdeeds.

Plastered against a green box that controls some of the street lighting in the area around Chicago and Washtenaw Avenues is the face of a young woman with exotically fashioned eyebrows and eyes and a comely smile. The purpose of this face is to announce a "beauty pageant" and "a garden of rabbits" at the Fireside Bowl.

The sign offers no further information, but it doesn't take long to find the Fireside Bowl, which is a bowling alley and music club—the "one established concert hall in the city that regularly hosts all-ages punk concerts," noted the *Tribune*—that sits on Fullerton Avenue near Rockwell Street. No one waiting to get into the club one night had anything to say when shown a picture of the face, though a couple of people remarked on its attractiveness. No argument there. It's an artful ad, and it fits perfectly on the green box. But it is, nevertheless, evidence of a crime.

POST NO BELLES

No cop is about to track down the person (or persons) who put the sign on the green box. There are bigger crooks to be nabbed. But you know who you are, and you are a criminal. It will come as news to the many hundreds of otherwise law-abiding citizens who have at one time or another plastered a wall or light pole with signs announcing yard sales, lost dogs, housecleaning services, and concerts, but they also have been breaking the law and could face stiff fines. They are criminals.

There is an ordinance, section 10-8-320 in the City of Chicago Municipal Code, that spells this out: "No person shall post, stick, stamp, tack, paint or otherwise fix, or cause the same to be done by any person, any sign, notice, placard, bill, card, poster, advertisement or other device calculated to attract the attention of the public, to or upon any sidewalk, crosswalk, curb or curbstone, flagstone or any other portion or part of any public way, lamppost, electric light, traffic light, telegraph, telephone or trolley line pole, hydrant, shade tree or tree-box, or upon the piers, columns, trusses, girders, railings, gates or parts of any public bridge or viaduct, or upon any pole box or fixture of the police and fire communications system."

Offenders can be ticketed, fines imposed: "not less than $10.00 nor more than $50.00 per pole for a first offense, and not less than $50.00 nor more than $200.00 per pole for any subsequent offenses." (Some suburbs have similar ordinances and penalties.)

How easy is it to find offenders?

After a walk of only six blocks, there she was. On Roscoe Street, a woman—a twenty-five-year-old sales rep for a pharmaceutical company—was observed taping an eight-by-ten piece

of paper to a light pole. "I'm looking to give away some kittens and thought this would be a good way for me to let people know," she said.

She was gently informed about the laws concerning the posting of bills. Her immediate reaction was shock.

"I can't believe the police would arrest me over this," she said, taping the piece of paper to the pole. Her sign contained a crude but not unappealing drawing of seven kittens and the words CUTE KITTENS *FREE* TO GOOD HOMES along with a phone number.

A week later, the sign was gone, along with others the woman had taped to a dozen or so poles on Roscoe as well as a couple on Halsted Street. Was that good? Did it mean that the kittens had found "good homes"? Or had the woman panicked and removed the signs herself, fearful of the law?

She and most of the people—such as the fans of Eric Fost, whoever he is—who commit bill posting do so innocently. But that is not true of the group known as the Campaign Sign Gang. When we enter election seasons, start looking around. The city will be filled with campaign signs, taped and stapled everywhere, affixed to any "lamppost, electric light, traffic light" and, if one could be found, "trolley line pole." Most of those who post political campaign signs know the legal ropes.

"Sure, we know it's illegal," says one campaign worker who is involved in a statewide race. "I don't know of anyone who's been fined, but most of us still do our work at night. Why take any chances?"

Some of the most hardened members of the Campaign Sign Gang insist that they are actually making the situation better because "we take down the signs of other candidates and put them in the garbage." Tell it to the judge.

Some citizens argue that the signs are part of what turns people off on politics. Many consider them, rightly, eyesores.

Campaign posters are among the most prosaic forms of street signage. Their messages are generally mundane—THE RIGHT CHOICE—and the faces of politicians rarely offer aesthetic pleasures. That is not true of the face of the nameless and lovely young woman used to herald the Fireside Bowl event. But when winter comes, with its harsh weather, her face and those of candidates (and lost dogs) will start to fade, then to vanish. And with evidence so effectively destroyed, the criminals will continue to wander free.

SEPTEMBER 27, 1998

CLEAN MACHINES

ON ONE OF THE COLDEST DAYS of the winter, Osgood and I found ourselves cruising east on Sixty-third Street. As we crossed Austin Avenue, we were transfixed by the sight of airplanes coming in low from the southeast to land at Midway Airport. But we were equally captivated by a large and busy car wash.

It is called the Spirit of America Car Wash, at 5115 West Sixty-third Street. That's as wonderfully appropriate a name as one could slap on such an establishment, for there is nothing more American, it seems to me, than our love affair with cars. And since Osgood's car had been seriously ravaged by winter, we decided to partake of the Spirit of America's services.

This place is vastly different from the increasing number of car washes that cater to the needs and vanities of the Volvo/Saab/SUV crowd. Some of those places call themselves "spas" and are so hands-on attentive to automobiles that I'm surprised they don't offer to massage the seats. The Spirit of America is no-nonsense. It is without frills. It has ten open bays, eight of them of the do-it-yourself variety. Its most expensive wash is seven dollars, which is barely enough to get your windows cleaned at some of the spas.

"I like to keep my car as clean as I can," said Hector Perez, braving the elements in one of the do-it-yourself bays. "Makes me feel good to have a clean machine."

There are some twenty-two thousand car washes in the United States, some eight hundred of them in the Chicago area with names such as Dirt Busters, Happy's Fast Hand Car Wash, Finishing Touch Auto Spa and Detail Salon, and Mr. Car Wash Ltd.

We were not up to washing the car ourselves and so waited in the automatic line behind a sleek limousine driven by a young woman. We paid our seven bucks and entered the bay. It was an otherworldly clime, with ice sculptures created by the combination of spraying water, soap, and wax with frigid temperatures.

And for a time, Osgood's car sparkled, and we both felt somehow less shabby than we had only minutes before. Conversation was more animated. Hey, we felt good. But, alas, it didn't take long before the salt and snow of the streets began to attack the car, and by the time we reached downtown, we were just two passengers in a grimy victim of another cruel and wicked Chicago winter.

FEBRUARY 27, 2000

NINE LIVES TO LIVE

IN MANY CHICAGO NEIGHBORHOODS, the presence of a stranger is cause for if not some alarm at least considerable interest. But few in the West Side neighborhood around Roosevelt Road and Waller Avenue have paid much attention to the stranger in their midst. Most are not even sure when he or she (or it) first appeared. But there it is, a cat, some fifteen or so feet tall with a blue necklace from which hangs a green shamrock pendant bearing the name Carl.

"He's ancient history," said Winfred Street as he waited for his lunch to go at Captain B's Shrimp House, one of the businesses in a strip mall across Roosevelt Road from the cat. "I'd say it's been here for about a year, more than a year. What do I think about it? Well, I kind of like it. It's a symbol, something different."

It also serves a practical purpose. "When I'm giving people directions," said Street, "I always tell them, 'Just look for the cat.'"

Another neighborhood resident, a guy in his thirties riding a children's bicycle, offered this wildly implausible explanation of the cat: "She's been here for seven months, I'd say. It used to be inside a store near here where they sell cats without a pet store license. They have hundreds of cats, and the big cat is how people find the store."

In the distance to the north sits Chicago Studio City, the city's largest film, video, TV, and commercial production facility. Ron De Rosa is one of the company's managers and knows all about the cat. He told us it is a former TV star, part of a float in a St. Patrick's Day parade that was filmed for the deceased CBS TV show *Early Edition,* which was set in Chicago.

"After that we kept him in different places," said De Rosa. "We finally decided to put him on the corner last year. We thought it would make a nice conversation piece."

That it does. It's a handsome cat with gentle eyes. But some people have pelted the cat with rocks, mistakenly believing that it was put there by the FBI and has "secret cameras" inside. Hey, folks, now that you know the truth, how about leaving the big kitty alone?

OCTOBER 13, 2002

HEALING AND HOPE

THERE ARE ONLY ABOUT FIVE THOUSAND Cambodians living in Chicago, and yet they—and all of us—have a most amazing new museum. The Cambodian American Heritage Museum, at 2831 West Lawrence Avenue, is an example of how ambition, hope, and perseverance can result in something of a miracle.

It has taken nearly three decades for this place to become a reality, but the efforts have been worth it. The museum's centerpiece, the Killing Fields Memorial, is a gathering of eighty glass walls of varying heights. Each represents twenty-five thousand lives, and etched in the glass are the names of relatives of Illinois Cambodians who died during the nightmarish regime of the Khmer Rouge in Cambodia between 1975 and 1979. It is estimated that as many as three million people perished as a result of starvation, torture, or execution in a country that has yet to fully recover.

The glass panels constitute the first such memorial in the United States, and, like the Vietnam Veterans Memorial in Washington, D.C., it is emotionally overwhelming in its simple presentation, which includes a stone column with the words WE CONTINUE OUR JOURNEY WITH COMPASSION, UNDERSTANDING, AND WISDOM.

It shouldn't be surprising that nearly 70 percent of the $1.5 million raised for the project came from this area's Jewish community, which knows a great deal about inhumanity and horror and losing loved ones.

Leon Lim, the chairman of the museum and the man featured in Osgood's photo, calls the museum "a place to educate, to heal, and to celebrate." He is looking at the names of nearly two dozen of his own relatives and friends etched in one of the glass walls. Though the Killing Fields Memorial, and some related exhibits, evoke deadly times, there is life aplenty in the museum in the form of literacy classes, cultural programs, language classes, and other building blocks for a hopeful future in this foreign land.

NOVEMBER 27, 2005

BIG BIG MAN

THERE IS NO TELLING what he would see if he could see, this forty-foot-tall, colorfully painted Indian who stands at Southwest Highway and Meade Avenue in Oak Lawn. But anyone who sees him does not soon forget him.

"He is an icon. Everybody knows him, and if they don't, they notice him," says Jim Shirazi, who owns the Cardinal Liquor Barn, in front of which the Indian stands.

There are dozens of these Big Man statues around, remnants of an era in advertising that predated Web sites and infomercials. It is even possible to get into heated debates about the area's gigantic creatures.

"I've never seen a Big Man as good as this," says Kathy Vukas, who works in the store. "It's a lot better than the one on Sixty-third and Pulaski," referring to a comparatively shabby Indian statue atop an eye care center in Chicago.

It's hard to argue with her. This is the best of the Big Men that Osgood and I have encountered. He was carted by crane to his present spot last October, when the liquor store moved into bigger digs. He originally stood, for at least thirty years, a block up the street in front of a bygone liquor and cigar store.

"I sometimes worry that there will be a car crash, so many people stop because of him," says Shirazi.

Those who do stop find a well-stocked and handsomely arranged liquor store with a great selection of fine wines. They also encounter a very nice dog named Vukey, a Labrador–border collie mix who is in the picture with Shirazi and who belongs to Vukas and her husband.

"Everybody loves Vukey," says Shirazi. "They love the Indian, too. People ask if I would sell the Indian. Never, except maybe one day at auction at Sotheby's."

APRIL 29, 2001

THE MAN ON THE PORCH

AMONG THE NOTABLE ARCHITECTURAL DETAILS of the Lakeside Inn, which sits atop a bluff across from the water in Lakeside, Michigan, is its hundred-foot-long front porch. It is a porch where, when the weather is fair, you'll find rocking chairs and a couple of swinging couches. It is a spot that compels contemplation and relaxation.

The porch is a place where Devereux Bowly Jr. likes to sit and stare out into the trees across the road and to the lake beyond. He lives most of the time in Hyde Park, but he owns the Lakeside Inn and the nearby Gordon Beach Inn, and being the ardent lover of buildings and history that he is, he cares for each of them as if they were his homes, too.

"I remember coming up here from the city many years ago as a teenager. How could you not be impressed?" Bowly says with youthful enthusiasm. "I loved it here."

In talking to Bowly about porches, one might never guess that he is an expert on architecture of a less gentle sort. His 1978 book, *The Poorhouse: Subsidized Housing in Chicago, 1895–1976,* is regarded as the best thing ever written on the often sorry subject.

A lawyer by trade, he first bought a summer home in this area in the 1980s. In 1991 he bought the Gordon Beach Inn in Union Pier at a foreclosure sale and, after having some success with that property, purchased the Lakeside Inn in 1994. Even then it was more than a century old, with a storied history best read about in a brochure or at www.lakesideinns.com. He has since restored the place, making it a popular vacation spot in all seasons. There is a private beach ninety stairs down (and up!) the dune on which the inn sits, and there are thirty-one rooms inside. The lobby is filled with wicker, and the stone fireplace is a sight to behold.

It is, in short, a place of great comfort, especially for a man who has invested so much of his time cataloging city structures where the comforts have been few and the living has most definitely not been easy.

NOVEMBER 17, 2002

BIKING IN BLIZZARDS

RIDING A BIKE IN THE CITY is an increasingly precarious pursuit, even when the weather is cooperative. On the nicest spring, summer, and fall days, the bike paths are jammed with pedalers and all manner of other amateur athletes, such as skaters and skateboarders and even those practicing the old-fashioned pursuit of jogging or the ancient activity of walking.

A few days after the winter's first blizzard, Osgood and I noticed a couple of bikes attached to a metal rack in front of the Carling Hotel in the 1500 block of North LaSalle Drive, and we decided to have a closer look. He, of course, saw this as an opportunity for an artistic photo. I, however, saw it as an example of a relatively new form of urban idiocy, as in, Who would be idiotic enough to ride a bike in winter?

One of the residents of the hotel came outside to see what we were doing, asking, "What are you doing?"

We said we were taking pictures of the bikes.

"What, some kind of art statue thing?" he asked.

Sort of, we said.

The man did not know who the bikes belonged to and said, "I doubt they're the bikes of people who live here."

"Why is that?" I asked.

"Most of the people I know here don't seem crazy enough to ride no bikes in the snow," he said.

But a large number are so inclined. Winter bike riding is growing in popularity. People in the industry will tell you so, but so will careful observation; even on the coldest, snowiest days, the bikers are about in high numbers. Much of this has to do with such recent technological developments as Gore-Tex and other fabrics that enable people to comfortably exercise outdoors without risking frostbite and the discovery that the tires used on mountain bikes work pretty well in the snow. (Why anyone who lives and rides in the Chicago area would need a mountain bike is a topic for another time.)

That all makes sense. But I rather think that much of this winter bike riding trend has to do with macho impulses. It's difficult to know. One of the problems with interviewing winter bikers is that they are moving very swiftly, as if dissatisfied with the depth of the windchill or in search of some private and altogether mysterious inner warmth.

JANUARY 14, 2001

A BLOODY GOOD PUB

THE LATE JOHN CORDWELL did not like to refer to the Lincoln Avenue business he owned as a tavern or as a bar, saloon, gin mill, or any of the other charming and colorful labels we associate with the thousands of places in the Chicago area that serve booze. He liked to call his place a pub, and when he opened the Red Lion Pub across the street from the Biograph Theater in 1984, the owner of the previous business located there, at 2446 North Lincoln Avenue—a "Wild West saloon" called Dirty Dan's—told Cordwell, "You're nuts. You'll be out of business in ninety days."

That was not such a wild assertion. Cordwell took all sorts of what could have seemed foolhardy steps: removing a jukebox and some video games; filling his menu with such oddities as Welsh rarebit, sausage rolls, and steak and kidney pie; and offering such then-exotic liquid refreshments as Bass, Watney's, and Whitbread.

Naturally, the decor bespeaks heavily of Britain, where Cordwell was born. But the posters, pictures, maps, and such that hang about look more as if they came from someone's attic than like a consciously constructed theme. This is not a place of gimmickry, hustle, and hype.

The Red Lion quickly attracted a steady clientele—in large part, I like to think, because Cordwell was almost always sitting somewhere inside, and there were few more pleasant barroom experiences than spending time with him. He was less owner than host, often with a twenty-year-old port in a glass beside him and his conversation peppered with phrases such as "filthy bugger" and "bloody" this or that. He might tell you about his native England, his service in the Royal Air Force, his capture by the Nazis, and what it was like to be a POW. He might talk about working years before as the city's director of planning or being one of the chief architects for the Sandburg Village complex or the builder of dozens of other smaller projects and homes. He was a civilized man in a civilized place.

Cordwell died in 1999, and though there are some who believe that he is among the many spirits who find the 1882 building a hospitable afterlife haunt, I have never encountered his ghost. But in his kid Colin—that's him in the British phone booth in the pub—one can hear John's laughter and feel his generous spirit and his passion for running a good, lively establishment, no matter what you call it. Or, as John would say, "This is a pub, and a bloody fine one."

JANUARY 11, 2004

A COUPLE OF DAYS after Osgood took this lovely shot of the city from 7600 south, I returned alone to Rainbow Beach. I did this because the beach was again, for about the sixth time this summer, closed to swimming and wading due to high levels of *E. coli* bacteria in the water. On this day, no other beach in the city was similarly affected. All the other beaches were open, and people were, presumably, happily splashing in their waters.

There were few people about—the sand and nearby park were not off limits. It was early morning. A couple of women walked their dogs. All manner of joggers, skaters, and bicyclists drifted by, most of them headed north toward the skyline that shimmered in the distance. For

SOMEWHERE

such a nice morning, it was surprising that people were not in a sunnier, more talkative mood.

"I'm not supposed to talk to strangers," said a little boy when I said hi. His mother said, "That's right, honey," and hand in hand they walked away.

Sick as the water may have been, it looked inviting, as did the whole scene. I hadn't been to Rainbow Beach in many years, though I have always admired its colorful name; other than the North Side's Kathy Osterman Beach, it's the only one of the city's sixteen major and sixteen minor beaches not named, prosaically, after the thoroughfares that lead to them. Decades ago, this was Chicago's most popular beach, but as the neighborhood around it got down on its heels, the city ignored the beach and allowed it to fall into a shabby and unappealing state. A recent multimillion-dollar facelift has transformed it into one of our loveliest beaches.

But the water was off limits, and at a concrete table a woman and three kids, none older than about five, were sitting as she patiently explained that they could not go in the water. At first they were whiny and upset, but she eventually distracted them by making them look "at all the big buildings out there" in the distance.

"What are they?" said one of the boys.

"That's the city," said the woman.

"Can we go there?" he said.

"One day," she said. "One day soon."

The kids' attentions turned to a gull trying to perch on the glass globe atop a light pole, and for a moment the city's skyline seemed so remote and strange that it might as well have been Oz.

SEPTEMBER 17, 2000

32

MAKING A SPLASH

WE ARE ALWAYS SEARCHING for something new and exciting, and a few weeks ago Osgood and I got more than we could have imagined when Millennium Park made its splashy debut. Even columnists and editorial writers went wild for the place. Osgood shot pictures, and I hung around watching kids smile into the Bean, roll on the grass, and say, as did one little girl in a pink dress, "They don't have something like this in Wisconsin."

There were concerts and street performers and a few very rich people whose checkbooks helped build the park and create the things in it. There were also tourists, a lot of them, and though most were there for the specific purpose of seeing the park, some claimed they were going to explore the city later. That meant, of course, trips to Navy Pier or window shopping along North Michigan Avenue. Some more adventurous types were going to wander the Loop. We talked to dozens of people, and not one of them expressed any interest in visiting what Osgood and I consider the gem of Grant Park. What, we should have asked these people, is the matter with Buckingham Fountain?

Undeniably, many of us who live here have come to take the fountain for granted, giving it a glance when cruising along the Outer Drive.

The fountain was formally dedicated on August 26, 1927, and its birthdays are now occasions not likely to get media coverage or even be noticed by any but the most ardent architecture or history geeks. But know that the fountain was a big deal when it made its debut. A gift to the city from Kate Buckingham, whose family made its fortune in grain elevators and banking, it was built as a memorial to her brother, Clarence. It was designed by Edward H. Bennett, who also helped design Wacker Drive and the Michigan Avenue Bridge.

On that long-ago August night, as water soared 135 feet into the air, John Philip Sousa led his band in "Stars and Stripes Forever" and fifty thousand Chicagoans stood and cheered in wonder. It's a wonder that it is still there. It's a wonder, period.

AUGUST 22, 2002

JUST PLAIN FOLK

EVERYBODY LOVES FRED HOLSTEIN. Whenever his name is mentioned, people of a certain age with a fondness for folk music will react with a smile and a "How is Fred?" Such is the result of a lifetime spent singing and sharing songs.

"I'm a ballad singer," Holstein says, standing in Sterch's, the Lincoln Avenue saloon where he works and where, in the photo, he's being hugged by the bar's owner, Bob Smerch. "What I really like is sing-along stuff. You hear the audience come back at you. It can be magical."

Magical, too, was a place called Holsteins. A few blocks north of Sterch's on Lincoln, it was, from 1981 to 1988, arguably the best folk music club in the country. Operated by Fred and younger brothers Ed and Alan, native South Siders all, it was a lively and creative place, and on the night it closed, the final song was a sing-along version of "For All the Good People."

That song—recorded live at the time—is among more than thirty tunes available for listening (and remembering) on a new two-CD release titled, with charming simplicity, *Fred Holstein: A Collection*. It's his first CD. He cut a record in the 1970s and another in the 1980s but nothing since, and fans have played the vinyl so often that the records have just worn out.

Such a person was Jules Eberhardt, who, along with WNUR-FM's Kathy Kelly, put together the new CD. It's a remarkable work that combines remastered tunes from the two LPs, songs from the archives of WFMT-FM, and even snippets of interviews Holstein gave over the years.

Fred performs rarely these days; there just aren't enough hospitable venues. But the CD will evoke such bygone places as the Earl of Old Town, Mother Blues, and Holsteins . . . an era.

"It took me a long time to learn it's not about me," says Holstein, who adds that he never could "get the hang" of writing his own songs. "I'm an interpreter, and what I do is about the songs, about the art, about the work. What I do is entertain people, and I use folk music as my way to do that. I see myself as a conduit."

I asked him where people could get a copy of his CD, and he said, charmingly old fashioned, "Any record store."

I asked Fred if he had a Web site where people could also order, and Fred said no.

"But it's right here on the CD, www.fredholstein.com," I said.

"Oh, right," said the folksinger. "I do have a Web site. What I don't have is a computer."

God love him.

AUGUST 5, 2001

36

IN THE CORN

IT TAKES ONLY A FEW MINUTES walking around the Farm-in-the-Zoo in Lincoln Park to realize that for most Chicago-area residents and tourists from big cities a farm is now as remote and exotic as the surface of Mars. With suburbs malled and paved with concrete, the farms that once dotted this area have all but disappeared.

Consider, then, the concept of the "entertainment farm." That is what Paul and Sherry Staley call their land, located near the towns of Paris, Elbridge, Marshall, and some other dots on the Illinois map, just west of the state line and the larger Indiana city of Terre Haute. The exact address of the farm, formally known this time of year as Pumpkin Works, is 21788 East Terre Haute Road. You really should think about going, driving the two hundred or so miles south and experiencing things that might make your kids forget all about video games.

The farming Staleys go back seven generations in the area. The barn that still stands on the farm was built in the 1850s by Paul's great-grandfather. But with family farming becoming an increasingly tough business, the Staleys decided in 1993 to embellish their pumpkin patch sales by offering a straw maze and haunted house.

Now they really do have an entertainment farm. There is a general store where you can buy things like handmade baskets and grab a bite to eat. You can pick pumpkins, Indian corn, and gourds; take an hour-long hayride across a hundred acres; sit by a campfire; pet some animals; climb a straw pyramid; visit a haunted dungeon; or play with a pumpkin slingshot.

But the real draw is the mazes. There are nine of them, from simple little straw structures for the kids to some that cover eight acres. Osgood regretted that he did not have a helicopter at his disposal since it would have provided the perfect way to capture the mazes. But, ever inventive, he did shoot a photo of a maze. Look closely: it's there on Paul Staley's hat. It's new to the farm this year, created in June and dedicated to the nearby 1544th Army National Guard unit. Its members are in Iraq, and one can only hope that when they sleep they dream of fields of corn, haunted houses, and hayrides back home in Illinois.

SEPTEMBER 5, 2004

THE KIDS OF SUMMER

ALMOST EVERY DAY THIS SUMMER, Osgood and I have observed that many of the area's parks, museums, zoos, and baseball fields are filled with packs of kids, most of whom seem to be toting little backpacks and almost all of whom seem to be wearing wide smiles. We have started to call these groups, such as the one from Evanston's Chandler-Newberger Sports Camp in the photo, the Day Camp Kids.

We were never part of that crowd. For those of us of a certain vintage, there are no day camp memories. We came of age in an era in which most moms stayed home and in which, true or imagined, the city seemed safer. Kids were left to their own devices and imaginations, and summer days often began with a "Bye, Ma. We're going to the park."

"Be home before it gets dark," the mothers would say.

There is, I suppose, an exciting innocence to memories of these do-it-yourself day camps. But for all the adventures I remember having, I also have visions of many days spent doing little more than sitting on the porch reading comic books.

That's one reason, I think, for the increasing popularity of day camps, for their organized activities. Enrollment has risen at a steady 10 percent a year for the last decade, and there are now some nine million kids going to nearly nine thousand camps nationwide. The choices are stunningly wide. There are computer camps, golf camps, theater camps, chess camps, and science camps. Name an activity or interest and there is almost certainly a day camp to fit the bill, though I've yet to hear about dentistry day camps.

But kids will always be kids, and the things that have not changed through the decades are the sounds: the giggles during a game of tag, the squeals at handling a snake or frog, the crack of a bat against a ball.

Wait, check that last one. The bats are now mostly aluminum, and when they hit a ball, the sound is more *plink* than *thwap*—and, for some of us, kind of hollow.

JULY 29, 2001

ONE VERY BIG BAT

ALL THESE YEARS LATER, standing across the street from 600 West Madison Street, memory drifted back to 1977. On a chilly April day that year, a young reporter stood on the corner. The area was still very beaten up, although the wrecking ball had begun its demolition of what was then our skid row, a stretch of cheap hotels, saloons, and sad souls clinging to what was left of life. One man, a recent and good customer of a neighborhood saloon, sidled up to the reporter and coughed a mean cough.

"Do you have anything to say about that sculpture?" the reporter asked the man.

The man grunted.

"I have something to say," said the man, his voice a rasp.

"Okay then," said the young reporter, his pencil poised against paper.

"Give me a dollar," said the man, "and I could build something better than that."

The "that" to which he was referring was *Batcolumn*, a 101-foot-tall work of pop artist Claes Oldenburg unveiled that day. Ever since, it has generated strong opinions. I have always found it charming, and Osgood was quite taken with the ways in which the sunlight plays off its open latticework and its crisscrossing diamond pattern is reflected on the windows of the Harold Washington Social Security Center.

Oldenburg is a Chicagoan. He graduated from the Latin School in 1946 and later attended the School of the Art Institute. He spent time in that legendary training ground for journalists, the City News Bureau. He was commissioned in 1975 under the General Services Administration's Art-in-Architecture Program to place contemporary American art in new federal buildings. (The city's first GSA artwork was Alexander Calder's *Flamingo*, erected on Dearborn Street in 1974.) He settled on a bat, saying that it was a monument "both to baseball and to the construction industry."

Oldenburg has always had interesting ideas about urban art, about his hometown. At a 1995 retrospective in Los Angeles, he displayed models of his visions for a massive fireplug at the east end of Navy Pier, the Daley Plaza Picasso sculpture as a giant cuff link, and the Tribune Tower as a huge clothespin. All we are likely to have is his bat. As Osgood took pictures of it from various angles, a man in a suit walked swiftly by and said, "You know what that bat needs is a huge ball."

MARCH 14, 1999

HOT COFFEE, COOL CATS

PERHAPS DON SELLE WAS CRAZY to open Don's Coffee Club on a leafy stretch of Jarvis Avenue in Rogers Park in 1993. The neighborhood was, he recalls, "wild, wilder than anything I'd ever seen." Perhaps he is crazy still, though the area has lost some, but not all, of its unsavory peppering of hookers, gangbangers, and drug addicts.

"I just make enough to pay the bills," says Selle, who shares an apartment above the Coffee Club with three cats. "I like to think of this place as my living room," he says. "When I opened, people said, 'Nobody goes out at night in this neighborhood.' That was only because they had no place to go. I have made so many good friends."

Don's Coffee Club recalls the city of a few decades ago, a city studded with storefront outposts: coffeehouses, theaters, bars. But in this age of homogeneity and franchises, Don's Coffee Club is wonderfully bohemian, in the best sense of that often misused word. It is a narrow, rectangular space randomly furnished with worn but comfy couches and armchairs. There are tables, lamps, ashtrays, artwork, and photos. "The decor? It is junk," Selle says. "Almost everything in here I got at junk stores. The rest came from neighbors just giving me stuff."

Don's offers none of the familiar liquids that fuel contemporary urbanites. There's no espresso, cappuccino, iced decaf mocha latte, or any of those other trendy caffeine concoctions. He's got coffee, regular and decaf, served in fine china or big cups; desserts and some meals, along the simple lines of peanut butter and jelly sandwiches.

Customers will answer the telephone if Don is otherwise engaged. They bring in desserts to share with patrons. They read books, write letters, argue politics and art, browse record albums: sounds of Benny Goodman, Artie Shaw, Billie Holiday, and the marvelous rest. Cats wander about, and sometimes when darkness falls a raccoon family—a mother and five babies—appear near the tables that sit on the sidewalk outside and wait for Selle to bring them food and water.

The neighborhood is starting to show signs of gentrification. How long before Starbucks starts sniffing for a corner on which to settle? Selle doesn't worry about such things. He loves what he does, and he's a great guy, charming. He'll drink coffee with you, but he's strictly a decaf man. "Have been for four years," he says. "My regular coffee makes me insane."

JULY 4, 1999

AND NOW

I FIRST MET BOB DANON more than thirty years ago when we worked for a magazine called the *Chicagoan.* I wrote stories and he was the circulation manager, and when the publication folded after eighteen months—through no fault of ours, I happily add—we went our separate ways. His way has been more circuitous than mine. I have mostly written stories, while Danon has done all sorts of things.

"Well," he says, "after the *Chicagoan,* I managed a restaurant for a couple of years and then I ran a framing shop on Armitage and then . . ."

There is always an "and then" with Danon.

"And then," he says, "I moved to Colorado, where I got married and had a daughter and ran a frame shop and gallery and then opened a hot dog restaurant next door called Last of the Red Hot Lovers and then . . ."

He got divorced, got sole custody of his daughter, Katie, and returned to Chicago, where he "had a lot of part-time jobs so I could be a full-time father." He managed art galleries. He sold posters. Working out of his apartment, he sold art to corporate clients, such as Michael Jordan's restaurant.

In 1996 he settled down, so to speak, by opening a frame shop at 1126 Central Avenue in Wilmette. A couple of years later, he took over the barbershop next door and turned it into a gallery. His first exhibition featured the work of the legendary Chicago artist Rudolph Pen.

In July he turned the gallery into Charlie's Coffee House, with soups, pastries, sandwiches, and, of course, coffees. And, as you can see, there is still art on the walls. (That's Danon in Osgood's photo, having a chat with Charlie, his eight-year-old English springer spaniel.)

But Danon didn't—couldn't?—stop there.

He began Friday Night Live, an ongoing weekly folk/bluegrass concert series that would feature such stars as Ed Holstein, Al Day, Michael Smith, Corky Siegel, Buddy Mondlock, Don Stiernberg, and Megan McDonough. "There really isn't anything like this on the North Shore," Danon says. "It's a throwback to the sixties and seventies, just like you and me." It will warmly remind all of us of a certain age of the Earl, the Quiet Knight, Orphans, Holsteins, Somebody Else's Troubles, and the other great clubs that helped get us through the nights.

NOVEMBER 7, 2004

BARN AGAIN

IN THIS THROWAWAY AGE, recycling remains a nuisance for most of us. But it's being taken to an artful level by Jay Wikary, who for the last six years has been in the unusual business of putting old barns back in business.

A remodeling contractor for two decades, Wikary had watched dozens, perhaps hundreds, of the barns that used to dot the Chicago area get bulldozed or burned to make way for cookie-cutter developments and shopping malls. Then he got the chance to bid on taking down six barns on a five-hundred-acre property in Prairie Grove. Instead of trashing the old timbers and boards, he decided to reuse them, starting the American Barn Company and giving it a lovely, heartfelt slogan: "Bringing New Life to Old Wood."

The store is at 3808 North Clark Street, in the neighborhood where Wikary was born and raised and, he confides, used to sneak into Cubs games on the back of beer trucks. He bought the Clark Street building in 1979 when it was a "beaten-up mess" and has since transformed it into a woody wonderland. It's a two-story workplace and showroom for ABC's products: tables, benches, picture frames, birdhouses, bed frames, and almost anything else that can be made from fine old wood.

Wikary works with Dan Mousel and Paul LeBeau, and their craftsmanship and reverence for history show in every piece they produce for private homes and a growing number of businesses. Each is dated and signed and accompanied by photos and documents relating to the barn from which it came.

"So many people are tired of stuff they have to get rid of every few years," says Wikary. "They want something they can hand down to their kids. They want history in their homes."

A few weeks ago, Wikary was in Elgin, dismantling another barn. "It's a fine barn, great wood. You'd be surprised how many barns are still around this area," he said. He paused before continuing. Gone from his voice was the enthusiasm it contained only seconds before. "But still, for every barn that I'm able to get my hands on, fifteen of them are being destroyed for landfill. They are going fast."

OCTOBER 24, 2004

MEMORIES OF A BLUE BIKE

THE FIRST TIME I had a bike stolen was in 1964. It happened on a quiet stretch of Wells Street, just north of Eugenie Street. It was, of course, a summer day. It was shortly after three in the afternoon. I was coming out of the Economy grocery store with a Popsicle in my hand when I saw a very large teenager getting on my bike, which I had left leaning against a tree.

"What are you doing?" I asked.

"Taking your bike," he said.

"Why?" I asked.

"Because I want it," he said. He laughed, got on the bike, and rode off.

The bike that was stolen from me was a blue Schwinn with black handlebars and baseball cards between the spokes. There was no lock. In those days there were no locks.

A certain innocence was lost the day my blue bike was stolen. And now bicycle locks are as necessary as air in the tires. Many of them, made from complex metal alloys and coming in odd shapes, look capable of frustrating the cleverest crooks. The locks need to be good, for they are now protecting sleek Italian racing models and sturdy mountain bikes that cost as much as a used car. Such temptations are too much for crooks. FBI statistics have it that more than five hundred thousand bikes (valued at $130 million or so) are stolen every year in the United States. A study by the Kryptonite lock company found that Chicago led the nation's cities in thefts.

"You've really got to be very lucky or very careful not to ever have a bike stolen," said a police officer strolling a section of Lincoln Park. "They haven't made the lock that can stop a smart thief."

Or a brazen one. To bust many bike locks takes a pair of industrial metal cutters, the cop said. "And that's not exactly something you can hide in your pocket."

Imagine what sort of heavy-duty saw was used by the thief who sliced the bike rack in Osgood's photo, which sits in the busy plaza of a Wabash Avenue office building.

It's unlikely that Mayor Richard M. Daley has had a bike stolen, at least not recently. He loves to ride on weekends and when he's on vacation. He's really something of a bike nut and wants to encourage others to be. In 1991 he created a Bicycle Advisory Council and has tripled the number of bike path miles in the city to something in the neighborhood of three hundred.

So have a nice ride—and get a good lock.

MAY 16, 1999

50

OF THE DOZENS OF TIMES I have been to Arlington Park, the 1993 trip I took there with Mickey Rooney ranks as the most memorable, if only because on that day he told me, "I lost a two-dollar bet sixty-five years ago and have spent about three million trying to get it back."

Rooney, then seventy-three and dressed in a heavy wool suit despite the ninety-degree temperatures, was eager to expound on what he said was the latest in a long series of betting systems of his own design. The greatest system in the world, as he explained it, worked like this: "You go by the morning line and find the horse among the top three picks that finished the farthest out of the money. You understand? If a horse finished seventh in his last race, what should his odds be? Six or seven to one? You understand? Why are they five to two? You see? There it is. You bet that horse."

AND THEY'RE OFF

Don't worry if you don't understand. Rooney did not win money that day.

Osgood and I go to the track a lot. "And some days I never want to leave," Osgood says. "This place is like a small town. Every time I turn around, something interesting's going on."

We have been there when the coat-and-tie crowd comes for the annual Arlington Million and on quiet weekdays when many people seem as interested in sunbathing as racing. We saw jockeys fall from their horses and listened as they tried to explain their unique sport. We watched longshots win and favorites fade. We met a lot of nice people, a number of odd characters and dreamers, hundreds of handsome horses, and some of the hundreds of people who care for them.

We realized that for most of the people who go to the track, it's only about the races, those two-minute (give or take) collaborations between human and horse, those bursts of muscle, energy, and speed in which people invest hope and money. The Kentucky Derby has long been called the greatest two minutes in sports.

Osgood and I rarely bet. We know that no one knows who will win a race, even though strangers, ushers, bartenders, and other racetrack denizens will tell you differently.

One of the raps against tracks is that they are gambling dens peopled by unsavory types. Or as James Joyce once put it, "The only decent people I ever saw at the racecourse were horses."

Granted, serious horse bettors are an odd breed, and you might meet one who is the cigar-chomping, garishly dressed, "I've got the horse right here" caricature. But that's an unfair image. Serious horse bettors, most of whom are dressed like golfers, are, on the whole, much friendlier

and less desperate than people you will find hunched hypnotically in front of the slot machines or leaning above the felt of the craps tables at casinos.

The best time to meet them is early in the morning, with the sun barely up and the day's races more than six hours away. The horse bettors who gather at this early hour will talk to you, though they will not likely share their names or strategies for selecting their day's picks. "This ain't like playing the lottery or one of the slot machines," said one white-haired early-morning fellow. "Where's the skill in that? I look at the horses, I talk to the trainers. I use my brain."

One person often among this crowd is Kurt Rittenburg, who was willing to talk to us and share his feelings and a few of his picks only because I have known him for forty years. A health care industry executive, he has spent a couple of days a week and almost every Saturday and Sunday for nearly twenty years at Arlington during its season. He sits in a box that he shares with family, friends, and clients. It rests on the finish line. He comes to the track with a copy of *Daily Racing Form* marked with different colored inks, personal hieroglyphics dating to the night before, when he handicapped the day's races. He bets a few bucks on most every race, more than a few bucks if he thinks the forms have divulged any secrets.

But he will tell you: "For me, this is about so much more than betting, than winning or losing. Look out there. Look at the skill and beauty. People just don't realize what tremendous athletes these horses and their jockeys are. There's so much effort and work in each race."

When he made the decision to purchase a seat at Arlington, he made a deal with himself. After each visit to the track, he would stop at a jewelry store in his Lincoln Square neighborhood and put down his winnings, if there were any, toward a surprise twentieth-anniversary ring for his wife, Carol. She got the ring in 1994, a few months early. So perhaps it's true, as Jane Smiley writes in *A Year at the Races: Reflections on Horses, Humans, Love, Money, and Luck*, that "every horse story is a love story" and "the racetrack is an inherently amazing place, rich in language and personality, sometimes beautiful and sometimes sordid, always unpredictable."

So look for me and Osgood at Arlington. Rittenburg too. Mickey Rooney, who certainly would have a new can't-miss system, might also show up.

MAY 5, 2005

DECADES OF GRUNTS

ONE NIGHT IN 1970 a young man named Richard Melman was sitting with his friend Jerry Orzoff and two young women. In anticipation of a free meal, Orzoff's date had eaten only an apple during the day. She was ravenously hungry, and halfway through the meal Orzoff turned to Melman and said, "This girl eats so fast she grunts."

The next year, the men opened a 102-seat restaurant at Lincoln Park West and Dickens Avenue and decided to call it R. (for Richard) J. (for Jerry) Grunts. The place was filled with what were then such novelties as a salad bar, a playful menu, and a blue-jeans-okay atmosphere.

Orzoff died in 1981, and sitting in Grunts one recent rainy afternoon, I was thinking about him and how happy he might be that Grunts was still around. For all of Melman's accomplishments—his Lettuce Entertain You Enterprises is one of the most successful restaurant companies in the country—the restaurant business is a bear, with failures far outnumbering successes. Indeed, in the summer of 1997, Melman announced that Grunts would close, citing rising rents and increasingly difficult parking in the area.

On the night of that announcement, I was sitting at the bar having coffee, tequila, water, and a vanilla milkshake—in separate glasses, of course—while watching a parade of former employees wander through the door.

"That's me," one of them said, pointing to a large picture of a pretty young blond woman, curls cascading down to her shoulders. "I don't look too bad now—for an old broad, that is."

It's amazing how something as ordinary as a restaurant can work itself so firmly under some people's skin. Maybe that's why owner Richard Melman decided at the eleventh hour to keep the place open. "It has always been important to me," he said, "but I wasn't aware of how important it was to others."

Not so very long ago Osgood and I sat in a wooden booth. We said hello to a wonderful waitress named Terry, who has worked there for more than twenty years. A couple of women in their forties told us they had not been in Grunts in more than a decade.

"It's nice that some things are constant," said one of them. "It's such a great . . . funky place. Can I say 'funky'? Oh, well. But what does it mean, R. J. Grunts?"

Wiping a white milkshake mustache off my face, I gladly took the time to explain.

FEBRUARY 18, 2000

MY LOVER THE CAR

REMEMBER YOUR FIRST CAR? Not the first car you ever bought but the first car in which you ever rode? For me that was a white Studebaker with shiny red seats that my father bought one day in the early sixties. That first ride was sort of like a first kiss, for in my youth cars were sexy. Consider this 1955 ad: "A realist might say that a young lady is more likely to arouse thoughts of love than an automobile. But a realist with such a literal outlook has never commanded a new Motormatic Chevrolet with a Turbo-Fire V-8 under its bonnet."

Okay, it's sexist, but you get the point.

Oddly, I have never bought a car. My cars have all been hand-me-downs: an exciting 1965 Mustang convertible that my brother left in my care when he went away to college and a stodgy four-door 1988 Ford that my mother passed on to me when she no longer had the patience for traffic jams.

But I love looking at cars, especially new ones, and I have always liked going to the Chicago Auto Show at McCormick Place. Frankly, the show is not as much fun as it used to be. I have no doubt that America's love affair with cars still smolders, but it has become muted. There's less passion. Going to an auto show used to be like going to a beauty pageant, a parade of sleek lines and big fins. Now it seems more like attending a power-lifting competition, with SUVs flexing their muscles.

Cars are not, of course, living things, but a few of the older ones have been able to achieve a wonderful and enriching immortality. For years local artist Jack Kearney scoured junkyards looking to buy car bumpers. With these and his own playfully creative vision, he fashioned animal sculptures that now embellish the city. (Personal favorites are the giraffes at Roscoe Street and Elaine Place.) But Kearney can't make any more of these because auto manufacturers long ago stopped using chrome to make bumpers, turning instead to lighter, less expensive, safer, and, let's face it, less sexy materials. There are more than 125 million cars being driven on North American highways. Every year 10 million vehicles are scrapped, recycled in various ways that are good for the environment—or at least better than in the past.

But every time I pass an auto graveyard, I remember my first ride and get a little sad. I fight this feeling by trying to imagine that all the dead cars, like those in the photo stacked at Cozzi Iron and Metal, were once polished and caressed and, perhaps, even beloved.

FEBRUARY 17, 2002

GIVING BACK

THOUGH REGARDED AS a great photographer, Osgood started his career as a reporter, and when we found a wonderful store called Casita Azul, at 817 Chicago Avenue in Evanston, we also discovered that Osgood had once written a story about its owner, Jill Negronida Hampton.

He wrote about her in 1995, when she, her sister Amy Negronida, their mother, and a business partner traveled to Mexico: "After a five-hour journey along a treacherous mountain road, a bus with 17 Mexican girls, four Chicago-area women and a missionary arrived by a full moon in the Mixe Indian village of Linda Vista in southern Mexico. The time was central standard, the lifestyle nearly first millennium."

That is good writing, and what the group was doing was a good thing: helping the people in the places that produced the goods that the women sold in their store, which was then in another Evanston location and called Ethnically Speaking. Osgood wrote of their visiting an orphanage with nine duffel bags filled with first aid kits, diapers, shoes, soap, balloons, and pen pal letters from kids at Evanston's Haven Middle School; of their trying, unsuccessfully it turned out, to find a site for a medical clinic. "The trip was incredible, fascinating," Osgood says.

Hampton closed Ethnically Speaking in 1999 and, after a few years selling goods on eBay, opened Casita Azul last October. "My sister really is a people person," said Amy. "The Internet really didn't fit her personality."

Amy said this while running the store one Saturday afternoon; her sister was on a buying trip in Mexico. The store is a colorful gathering of items priced from a couple of bucks to many hundreds of dollars for exquisite beaded creations by the Huichol tribe. There are also some colorful purses for sale. Ten percent of the revenue from these items helps support a 120-bed dormitory in Mexico for the families of people who have been hospitalized with serious illnesses.

"Jill's philosophy is to give back in any way we can to the artists and their communities," says Amy, who can been seen (on the left) with sister Jill in Osgood's fine photo.

OCTOBER 2, 2005

SPICY SURPRISES

YOU WOULD HAVE TO BE pretty hip to know the difference between Las Guitarras de Espana and Ten Part Invention, or the Paul Wertico Trio and Von Freeman, but you could raise your hipness IQ by going to see them, and others, at the HotHouse.

Born in Wicker Park in 1987 and, since 1998, located at 31 East Balbo Avenue, HotHouse has been called "the most beautiful club in the city" by *Chicago* magazine. And that lively publication *Barfly* has deemed it "a mecca, if you will, of artistic and musical diversity." We say it is one of the best clubs on the planet. In an era when many clubs serve the same entertainment "meals," the HotHouse menu is an eclectic explosion of films, forums, readings, and mostly music, a vast and varied offering full of spicy surprises.

Osgood and I went to see great local jazz singer Spider Saloff performing with Bill Sheldon and Tom Hope. The crowd for their show, *France—for Better or Verse,* was young/old/black/white/brown, which pleased Saloff. "It was great, so much more interesting than some of the clubs I've played," she said. "It's beautiful and gets such a diverse audience."

Running the eight-thousand-square-foot joint, which includes an art gallery, is Marguerite Horberg, known in some quarters as the older sister of film producer Bill, whose movie credits include *Cold Mountain, The Talented Mr. Ripley,* and *Searching for Bobby Fischer.*

"We have been growing with every year," says Horberg, who grew up with her brother on the North Side. "There are a lot of new residents in the area, a lot more activities at the nearby colleges [Columbia College and Roosevelt University]. We have started doing tie-ins with many of the city's free summer programs, such as SummerDance. Things are good and getting better. We've got a lot of irons in the fire, a lot of exciting new projects."

Such as? "This fall we'll be coming out with our first CD on the HotHouse label," Horberg says.

That's nice. You'll be able to buy it and listen to it at home. But do us a favor first: go listen at the club.

AUGUST 29, 2004

LITTLE BIG MAN

A SMALL MAN IN LIFE and now nearly forgotten unless his name is linked with Lincoln and debates, Stephen A. Douglas in death is a giant, standing atop a column that is atop his tomb at the center of a lovely little park on the Near South Side. Douglas has been at this place since his death in 1861. The Douglas Tomb State Historic Site has been at 636 East Thirty-fifth Street since 1881, when the State of Illinois appropriated funds for it.

"I love it here," says Rick Herbert, an affable thirty-seven-year-old seasonal worker for the state, which manages the facility. "I used to live down the street when I was a boy, and I was scared to walk by here. I thought it was a graveyard. Now I'm not scared at all. There is something spiritual about it."

Herbert, along with two men for whom he works, tenderly cares for the site.

"In the spring you should see the flowers," he says. "The whole park comes alive with colors."

Herbert is a former clothing salesman and the father of six children. He is an enthusiastic, delightful guide to the two-and-a-half-acre site. Most of the people who visit the Douglas Tomb are tourists. "There are a lot of people who live in the neighborhood who have never even been here," says Herbert. "Isn't that the way it sometimes is?"

True enough, but it is hard to imagine what might draw tourists to this spot, for Douglas is now regarded as a minor player in Illinois politics. In his time he was anything but. Born in Vermont, he arrived in Illinois in 1833. The twenty-year-old then built an incredible career: he was a lawyer, an Illinois secretary of state, and a congressman, and in 1846 he was elected to the U.S. Senate. The famous debates with Lincoln took place during Douglas's reelection campaign in 1858. Douglas won the election, but the debates brought Lincoln to national attention and eventually to the White House.

Douglas stood a few inches taller than five feet and was called the Little Giant. His monument stands very tall, ninety-six feet, with a nine-foot-nine-inch statue of him atop a forty-six-foot column rising above the tomb and granite base. The tomb is adorned with symbolic art and allegorical figures representing Illinois: Justice, History, and Eloquence. Douglas's body rests in a white Vermont marble sarcophagus that bears the dates of his birth, April 23, 1813, and his death, June 3, 1861. There is also this message carved into the marble: TELL MY CHILDREN TO OBEY THE LAWS AND UPHOLD THE CONSTITUTION. It is all the work of Leonard W. Volk, a well-known sculptor of the time and a relative of Douglas's through marriage. He did the Little Giant proud.

JANUARY 16, 2000

ETHAN'S LITTLE SECRET

YOU MIGHT THINK the bird in the photo is winking, sharing some sort of secret with Osgood. But the red-tailed hawk named Ethan is not winking. Rather, his distinctive look is the result of his having lost an eye five years ago. A kind person brought him to the Trailside Museum in River Forest, where he has lived ever since. What a wonderful if secret little spot this is, functioning not only as a wildlife rehabilitation center for orphaned and injured animals but as a nature center for increasingly out-of-touch-with-nature urban folk.

On the banks of the Des Plaines River at the intersection of Thatcher and Chicago Avenues, the Trailside Museum has been serving this area for more than seven decades—even longer if you count its previous lives. Its main building, constructed in 1874 and originally a finishing school for young ladies, later became a home for boys from broken families. It was purchased, along with the surrounding land, in 1917 by the Forest Preserve District of Cook County to serve as its headquarters. In 1931 it was converted to its present use.

Here you can find exhibits on native flora and fauna, observe and learn about animals such as Ethan, and hike the surrounding heavily wooded trails.

It is a unique property but not one without problems. A volunteer nonprofit group called the Trailside Wildlife Foundation has argued that the facility lacks sufficient funding from the county, and last year it proposed that a public-private partnership be formed to take over the operation of the place.

The proposal, last we heard, is under review by a county board committee. Osgood and I couldn't tell you how many members of that committee have recently visited the center, but we can tell you that all of them would benefit greatly from the trip.

APRIL 25, 2004

UNDERGROUND BOOKS

LAST YEAR THERE WERE nearly 175,000 books published in the United States, and on any given day it might seem as if all of them, as well as tens of thousands more published in previous years, are lining the shelves of the Seminary Co-op Bookstore, at East Fifty-eighth Street and University Avenue, in the heart of the University of Chicago campus.

It's an illusion, of course—the store has only about 110,000 titles—but a pleasant one, for there is no bookstore in this or any other neck of the woods that offers such delightful, surprising, and, perhaps, enlightening strolls through its mazelike subterranean space.

Where else might you find on just one foray such provocative titles as *The Racketeer's Progress: Chicago and the Struggle for the Modern American Economy, 1900–1940* or *White on Arrival: Italians, Race, Color, and Power in Chicago, 1890–1945* or *The Sexual Organization of the City*?

We have been going to this store and its outposts, 57th Street Books at 1301 East Fifty-seventh Street and the A. C. McClurg Bookstore in the Newberry Library at 60 West Walton Street, for decades and have been remiss in not thanking the man in Osgood's photo for so many hours of pleasure. He is Jack Cella, longtime manager of the original store who, along with thirteen other people, created it in 1961 when they each ponied up ten dollars toward the purchase of a hundred books and the rent on a basement space in the Chicago Theological Seminary (hence the name). It has since become internationally renowned and locally cherished as a book lover's paradise.

These are increasingly tough times for independent bookstores, whose numbers have been declining slowly but steadily since 1950. The American Booksellers Association says that such oases account for less than 20 percent of retail book sales. The chains, most prominently Barnes and Noble and Borders, account for about 30 percent, with the rest coming from mail-order book clubs, the Internet, and such mass-market merchandisers as Wal-Mart.

Amazingly, though it does not offer lattes, CDs, diet books, cards, and the other odd embellishments to be found at the chains, the Seminary Co-op thrives. It is a place that constantly makes readers rejoice. It is a place you should visit and wander.

OCTOBER 17, 2004

I'M A BIT OLD to celebrate St. Patrick's Day in the raucous manner of years past, and I admit I've lost the wonder I once felt when surrounded by people dressed from head to toe in green.

Tommy Nevin's Pub in Evanston will be jammed on St. Patrick's Day. There will be people eating, drinking, and celebrating. If you, too, can no longer find your KISS ME, I'M IRISH buttons, it might be a good idea to visit Nevin's on some Sunday.

For years now, the bar/music room at Nevin's, 1450 Sherman Avenue, has been the setting for informal gatherings of professional and amateur musicians who meet to share tunes.

"It's also about *craic*," said one who frequents the place, explaining that that word is an Irish term for conversation and good company.

SUNDAYS IN SALOONS

Spending part of a Sunday at Nevin's is to experience fiddlers, tin whistlers, singers, and Irish pipe players who are performing for the pure, companionable joy of it.

It is also to be reminded of Sunday afternoons long ago when little friends and I would venture the few blocks from our apartments to the Earl of Old Town on Wells Street for its kids-welcome Sunday shows. That is where, sipping Cokes, we would listen to such performers as Steve Goodman, John Prine, the brothers Holstein, Michael Smith, Bonnie Koloc, and so many others. Actually, I am not sure that I saw all those performers on Sundays at the Earl. But so much a part of my life has their music become that it is hard to imagine I wasn't seduced at a tender age, about the same age as the young man in Osgood's photo, an eleven-year-old named Farley Kelly. Though he is adept at wind instruments, some would argue he is more accomplished on the fiddle.

I envy him his talent, his future, and the ears of those who will be moved by his music on a St. Patrick's Day far in the future or another Sunday just around the corner.

MARCH 10, 2002

URBAN BEASTS

THIS IS THE CITY that gave birth to the skyscraper and a city that keeps building them at a furious pace.

A skyscraper, by definition in *Webster's New World College Dictionary,* is simple and vague: "a very tall building." What would William Le Baron Jenney make of the city's many very tall buildings? He designed the first skyscraper, the Home Insurance Building. It was ten stories high, built from 1884 to 1885, and razed in 1931 to make way for the Field Building, at 135 South LaSalle Street, which is now called the LaSalle National Bank Building.

Ten stories is a dwarf these days, and among the many things that have allowed buildings to grow ever higher is the contraption in Osgood's photo. One day, seeing a flock of them just west of the Museum Campus, we realized (and were more than a bit embarrassed by) how little we knew about these urban beasts that hover over the city.

What are they called?

"Construction cranes," said Osgood so tentatively that his answer almost begged a question mark.

That's close but not precise. They are tower cranes and are used to lift steel beams and all sorts of other equipment, such as generators. They arrive on trailers. The base is anchored to a concrete pad, and the components—mast, slewing unit, jib, machinery arm, counterweights, operator's cab—are then pieced together.

As the building grows, so does the tower, in twenty-foot increments by means of hydraulic rams. It's an engineering marvel, but have you ever seen it happen? We doubt it. We haven't. And that made us remember that decades ago the construction of a new building usually attracted hundreds of curious onlookers. Now we rarely see people watching buildings being built. Perhaps we take giant buildings for granted, the wonder of them sadly lost in their sky-scraping familiarity.

JUNE 13, 2004

UPTOWN GUY

THE BEST RESTAURANT you have probably never heard of is Frankie J's on Broadway, which has been serving great food, presenting interesting theater, and struggling mightily to get people in the door of the building at 4437 North Broadway. Since buying the building in 2001, Frankie Janisch has refashioned it, mostly on his own, into a theater and restaurant; gathered petitions that would allow him to serve liquor and hired lawyers to help with the process; and tried to attract customers by zealously promoting Uptown as an exciting neighborhood.

It has been a money-draining and spirit-sapping experience. "I've never given up at anything," says Janisch. "You bet this has been tough. I'm kind of down to my last nickel. But this has been my dream, and I will not let it die."

He is the youngest of six boys from Rogers Park, where he still lives, and he loves this town and its history. Near the entrance of the restaurant is a wall covered with photos and objects, an homage to Janisch's father, William, a Chicago firefighter for thirty-nine years.

"I see such great potential in Uptown," he says.

Frankie J's occupies a building built in 1892 as a church. It was later a funeral home, later an art gallery. In the 1970s, Janisch will happily tell you, it was the home studio of a porn filmmaker who was shot and killed there. His ghost is said to haunt the place.

Just before Janisch bought the building, it was a methadone clinic, a function that inspired the name of his MethaDome Theater, a fifty-seat space on the second floor, its antique wooden chairs salvaged from a church that was razed.

"The kitchen is my stage," Janisch says.

While his older brothers messed around with cars, Frankie was taught to cook by his grandmother. While in high school, he worked in local restaurants; he later graduated from the Culinary Institute of America and then cooked all over town. But he is also a comic. Before opening his "dream" in Uptown, he was the CFO of the ImprovOlympics.

He has been able to balance his cooking career with acting and improv studies and performances. He has been in some movies, plays, and many improv shows. His skills combined in *Frankie J Superstar on Broadway,* a show that included a three-course meal, cooking demonstrations of each course, musical parodies, and other surprises.

"I call it the first ever cooking show musical," Janisch says about this production, a deliciously ambitious undertaking.

APRIL 3, 2005

C'MON IN—REALLY

A WOMAN JOGGING on a day hot enough to bruise the brain had decided to rest on a small patch of grass directly in front of a building on the southwest corner of Diversey Parkway and Lakeview Avenue, at the edge of Lincoln Park. Like many people before her, she found the Elks Veterans Memorial beautiful but intimidating. "I've never even tried to go in," she said.

There are many buildings that do not issue invitations, that seem to say, "This is a place of serious business. You'd better have some if you're coming in here." But the Elks Veterans Memorial, one of the most majestic buildings in the city, welcomes the public: 9:00 A.M. to 5:00 P.M. weekdays and, from April 15 through November 15, 10:00 A.M. to 5:00 P.M. on Saturdays and Sundays.

Designed by New York architect Egerton Swarthout, the memorial was completed in 1926 at a cost of $3.4 million. Its interior columns, walls, and flooring are made of twenty-six types of marble. It is filled with sculptures and murals, a dozen of which adorn the building's hundred-foot-tall rotunda, along with four bronze human figures symbolizing charity, fidelity, justice, and brotherly love. An adjacent reception room contains more murals, chandeliers, and richly colored English and Scottish oak paneling.

A five-million-dollar restoration in 1997 gave the building a new shimmer. But it also contributed another, less appealing, element. *Tribune* architecture critic Blair Kamin assailed the white wrought iron fence that was added around the building as part of the restoration: 330 feet along Lakeview and 180 feet along Diversey. Kamin wrote: "Given the care lavished upon the restoration . . . this klutzy detail is nothing less than heartbreaking." This fence was built not to break hearts but to keep skateboarders from destroying the building's limestone steps.

The runner eventually stood up. Saying that she thought it would be "quiet and cool" inside the memorial, she jogged off into the sweltering open spaces of the park.

AUGUST 1, 1999

TWO STORIES, NO WAITING

GAYS IS A TOWN of about 250 people and one two-story outhouse.

Located forty-five miles south of Champaign and six miles west of Mattoon, Gays is a pleasant place, just a dot on any road map. But its outhouse—known as a "skyscrapper"—attracts a considerable number of tourists, who pull their cars off the road and snap photos of the building.

For many years the townsfolk proudly and with, it would seem to me, justifiable confidence claimed that this was the only such outhouse in the country. When that claim was reported in another newspaper, the citizens of Belle Plaine, Minnesota; Crested Butte, Colorado; Dover, Arkansas; and Phelps, New York, begged to differ. They, too, all had two-story outhouses.

Who would have known? Or imagined?

The Gays outhouse came into being when Civil War veteran Samuel F. Gammill built his general store in 1869. There were apartments above the store, and Gammill had the clever notion of a two-story outhouse to allow the apartment dwellers access without the need to traipse downstairs and stand in line with store customers. Gammill's design was brilliant. The holes on the top level (one for men and one for women, as was the custom) were set farther back than those on the ground floor. A false wall protected things. And it all worked swell for more than a century.

When the store was torn down in 1984, some residents fought to keep the outhouse, and a fellow named Pat Goodwin restored it. Now, with its pine boards painted white and its black shingles shining, it sits in a small park along Illinois Highway 16.

That's Pat's mom, Nancy, in Osgood's photo—which, by the way, was shot with a pinhole camera—holding a portrait of the outhouse when it was functional. She is village trustee and believes the outhouse is historically significant. I think she's right. It's an architectural oddity that provides a glimpse into the ways in which, at a most basic level, we all used to live.

AUGUST 17, 2003

SKULL SESSION

UNTIL ABOUT 1960, Lynn Duenow was a person without any obvious obsessions. But during that year, while Duenow was a student at the School of the Art Institute, he made frequent trips to the then-vibrant Maxwell Street market and there made a purchase that would help set the course of his career.

"I bought this skull nutcracker that had been made at the turn of the century," says Duenow, who teaches sculpture at New Trier Township High School in Winnetka. "Later I bought a small ivory carving of a skull."

And so it began. For nearly forty years he has devoted much of his own work and study to the images of skulls and death that most of us think about only around Halloween but that have been part of art, religion, and culture for centuries. When he talks about skulls and skeletons, he does so with an artist's passion and appreciation, talking about the history of art and speaking of "powerful symbolism" and "intensity of images."

He numbers his collection of skull items and art at about four thousand. Few would argue that the most personal of these is the one in his mouth, a tooth in the shape of a skull. "In order to stop smoking many years ago, I started drinking Coke like crazy, up to four quarts a day. That's what my dentist believes was responsible for my losing a tooth," says Duenow.

That was thirty years ago, and instead of having a conventional bridge, Duenow made a skull mold for a new tooth, and that's what was fitted in his mouth. It's visible only when he makes a point of showing it, as he graciously did for Osgood's camera.

At the end of the school year Duenow will retire and be able to devote more time to his own work. Already he is thinking beyond skulls to "etchings on mirrors, huge totem poles made from modern materials, and"—he adds enthusiastically—"tombstones."

OCTOBER 31, 1999

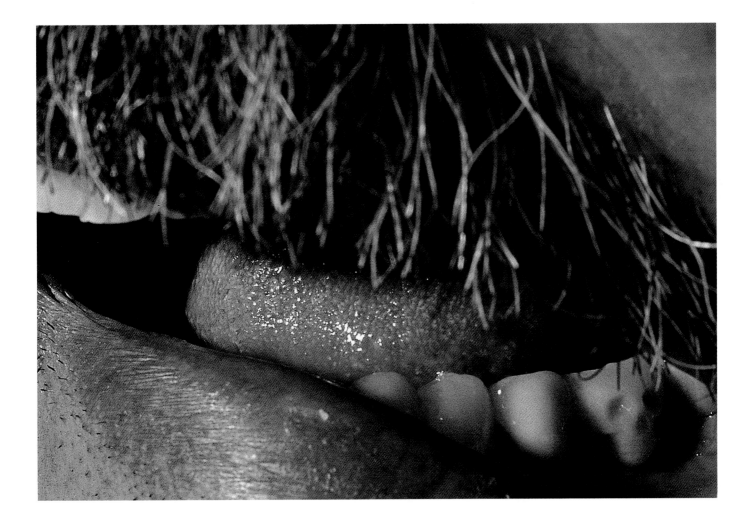

A LIFE IN THREE ACTS

IN THE 5200 BLOCK of South Greenwood Avenue, filled with hundred-year-old row houses, we found seven-year-old Rex Hughes sitting by a stone lion and, understandably, knowing nothing about the man who built the houses.

Samuel Eberly Gross, dead ninety years, is mostly forgotten. But he is one of our most influential and colorful characters. As Miles Berger writes in his 1992 book, *They Built Chicago: Entrepreneurs Who Shaped a Great City's Architecture,* "Without question, Gross was the most prolific homebuilder in Chicago history."

Gross claimed—and no one argued—to have built more than twenty subdivisions and ten thousand homes, sold more than forty thousand lots, and established more than fifteen towns or villages, many long since absorbed into the city. His most famous development is Alta Vista Terrace on the North Side. Built between 1900 and 1904, it was Gross's last major development, with homes selling for forty-five hundred to seventy-two hundred dollars. In 1971 it would become the first residential district to be designated a Chicago landmark.

Gross was born in Pennsylvania and raised, the oldest of seven children, in Carroll County in northwestern Illinois. He served in the Union army during the Civil War and afterward went to law school and was admitted to the bar in 1867. For the next seven years he bought land and built buildings, got married, and retired to a Gold Coast mansion in which he read and wrote voraciously and studied mathematics and science. By 1880 he was back in the real estate business. His target buyers were blue-collar folks and immigrants. His catalogs and ads touted his buildings as "the workingman's reward: a home for $10 a month."

Richard Christiansen, the former theater critic for the *Tribune* who has written a wonderful book about the history of Chicago theater, *A Theater of Our Own,* will tell you that Gross wrote the play *The Merchant Prince of Cornville.* The story of a good-hearted poet who courted a woman on behalf of a shy friend, it was performed in London in 1896, a year before the premiere of Edmond Rostand's *Cyrano de Bergerac.* In 1902 Gross sued Rostand for plagiarism. A Chicago judge ruled in his favor. A few years later, after divorcing his first wife, marrying a teenager, filing for bankruptcy, and moving to Michigan, Gross announced that he was planning to mount productions of *Cyrano,* which he had begun to describe as his play.

He never did build another building. He died in 1913 and was buried in Rosehill Cemetery.

AUGUST 24, 2003

A SCAR COURSES JAGGEDLY ACROSS a portion of Marc Smith's face, just below his right jaw. It is an old scar, growing faint, and only those close to Smith can see it. But no one is close to him now as he shouts from the stage of the venerable Green Mill Jazz Club near the shabby corner of Lawrence Avenue and Broadway: "I heard it on the roof. It rained today . . . Poetry is a sky dark with wild duck migration. Poetry is the heart of the people and the people is everyone. What everyone says is what we all say."

The audience, many of whom are still damp from a violent Sunday storm that has moved out over the lake, is a lively but attentive crowd. Young and old, white and black and brown and yellow, wealthy and paycheck-to-paycheck, it's the sort of urban mix that would make a populist proud. Most are drinking. All are here to see the Uptown Poetry Slam. It is Marc Smith's creation and, in its fashion, his ongoing salvation.

POETRY IN COMMOTION

"You know what's interesting about all the love poets who get up on this stage?" he says. "They always come alone."

He smiles a wicked smile. He's like Elmer Gantry, an audacious, exciting combination of showbiz and evangelical spirituality. And that has served him well over the many years that he has been the passionate pitchman/emcee of the Sunday night slam.

Smith describes the weekly event as "a grab bag variety show which mixes together an open stage, special guests, musical and dramatic acts." Its centerpiece—the slam itself—is a competition among poets scored by three judges chosen at random from the crowd. Audience members are encouraged to voice their displeasure with the poetry by finger snapping, foot stomping, groaning, hissing, or grunting. The winning poet gets ten dollars.

This hook, this gimmick—this slam—has made Smith's creation an international cultural phenomenon. Poetry slams now take place on a regular basis in more than a hundred U.S. cities and a number of foreign countries. The highly respected New York poet Bob Holman calls the slam "the most active grassroots arts movement in the country for the last decade," and Smith says, "It's not hard to understand the success of the slam. It's a crowd-pleaser."

In that crowd some see community. "In most bars people don't have anything really to say to one another," says Sheila Donahue, a slam veteran. "But the slam mixes people together, lets them get to know each other. The experience of going onstage is at once intimidating and

liberating. You see people being vulnerable, and there is reward in that. There is a sense of self-discovery, a sense of community."

It is onstage that Smith feels fully alive. It is onstage that Smith sheds his insecurities and doubts. "I am an entertainer," he says, and each Sunday he starts the slam with the words "I'm Marc Smith," and those in the crowd who know the routine respond with a collective "So what!?!"

Poet Cin Salach believes this represents an essential element of the slam. "No one can move a crowd like Marc," she says. "But humility makes it work. The slam isn't about being famous, being a star. Marc's humility—the 'So what!?!'—keeps it about poetry."

To watch Smith onstage is to see him alternately cajoling and encouraging, angry and soft, playful and pained. But he is always fiery and he is always attentive, even in the face of the most god-awful poetry. He appears born to his task, conductor of a word symphony of organized chaos. Seeing him in this setting makes it hard to believe that he was once a "person so shy that I had to have my wife call and order the pizza."

Poetry gave his emotions a voice. Performance liberated that voice. The slam community sustains him. But Smith will be the first to tell you that he did not invent the intermingling of poetry and performance. That has a lengthy, if spotty, tradition in Chicago, from poetry read to jazz accompaniment in the 1920s to 1960s poetry readings and even some competitions among poets. Today there are poetry readings in venues from bookstores to bars. What Smith did, almost by accident, was synthesize performance and poetry and create a hybrid that would satisfy the self-expressive needs of those willing to get up onstage and also would attract an audience willing to pay (five dollars at the Green Mill door) to hear those expressions. In so doing he found his own comfort and shelter, and each time he watches a poet—especially one who has never before read in front of a crowd—one imagines his mind floating back to a 1983 night and his own first public reading. It was his epiphany.

Now he says, "I don't consider myself close to being a good poet. But I have worked hard. I have paid my dues."

Lives are all about distant echoes, and the case could be made that poets are able to hear them with greater clarity than the rest of us. From the Green Mill stage, the echoes are allowed to take the form of words. Some of what is heard may sound like mere noise or nonsense. But some of it rises above. Some of it is true. Some of it is, really, poetry. And the audience seems to care.

NOVEMBER 23, 2003

FOLLOW THE BOUNCING BALL

SICK OF SURVEYS, are you?

Here are the results of a survey that has nothing to do with politics: table tennis, 481; Ping-Pong, 991. That is the number of mentions each of those has received in the *Tribune* since 1985, which is as far back as the paper's computerized archives go. The tally seems fitting, because this is still the kind of place where people prefer the less politically correct and proper "bowling alley" to "bowling center," "pool hall" to "billiard parlor."

Chicago has a gloried Ping-Pong past, but when the city put some three hundred Ping-Pong tables in lobbies, plazas, and other public spaces during the summer of 2000, it was met with derision from the media.

"What connects the City of the Big Shoulders and the game of little paddles?" a *Tribune* editorial demanded. "Actually, there is nothing wrong with a big city being a little silly sometimes. It shows it has confidence and a healthy sense of humor. But Ping-Pong?"

The *Sun-Times* also rapped the Ping-Pong idea, resulting in a flap with the mayor, who threatened to remove the table the city had placed on the paper's property.

Much of what rubs some people the wrong way about Ping-Pong is that they consider it a game rather than a sport. Try telling that to Chi Lee, in Osgood's photo captured in a fearsome and focused pose at the Chicago Chinese Table Tennis Club in the heart of Chinatown. There are often tournaments in Chicago, some attracting as many as forty thousand participants. I'm always tempted to go watch some of the action. I'm even tempted to say that Ping-Pong is the next big indoor sporting thing.

Recently, a health club put a table in one of its racquetball courts, and many mornings you can see a couple of high-ranking *Sun-Times* editors playing there, with increasing proficiency and ferocity and obvious delight.

OCTOBER 20, 2002

WHEN THE MOOD STRIKES

TONY FITZPATRICK, THE HIGHLY REGARDED artist, fine husband, devoted father, and former amateur boxer, started shopping at the G Boutique when it opened. Almost every day he walks from his studio across the street to buy Mood chocolate candy.

"That's why when we got some chocolate body frosting in, we had Tony taste it first," says one of the store's salespeople, Rebecca Fox, a young Northwestern University graduate who with some pals started a theater company called the Barstow Project. "We had to make sure it met his approval before we started selling it."

"I love the place," says Fitzpatrick, though he is loath to discuss what else he buys there, for most of the things the store sells fall into the category of unmentionables.

The G Boutique, 2131 North Damen Avenue, is refreshingly open about all things sexual. The brainchild of longtime friends Cheryl Sloane and Kari Kupcinet-Kriser, the store is, in Sloane's words, "a place where women could come to feel good about themselves."

Sloane and Kriser (left and right in the photo) know a lot of people. Sloane is the daughter of Joyce Sloane, producer emeritus of The Second City, and Kriser is the granddaughter of the indomitable newspaper columnist Irv Kupcinet.

Their store is a pleasant oasis that looks, at first glance, like so many of the warm and cozy shops in the neighborhood. It is filled with items made for encounters of the intimate kind: body oils and massage potions, books (a couple of titles on the shelves are *Zen Sex* and *Love Magic*), some jewelry, various electronic gizmos, and dozens of clothing items meant for the bedroom. Some of these are relatively conventional, while others are the sort most often found in men's fantasies.

The clientele is 70 percent women, but an increasing number of men are dropping by and buying a lot more than candy.

NOVEMBER 24, 2002

THE COLLECTOR

DAVID PHILLIPS WAS WORKING as the chief photographer for a chemical company in St. Louis in the early 1960s when he fell in love with Chicago. That love affair has been ongoing and passionate, and it has produced the most magnificent photo collection we've ever seen or ever will.

Phillips has spent his career searching out and buying old images, such as the two he is holding in Osgood's photograph: glass plate negatives of Michigan Avenue as it looked in the 1920s and a portrait of activist Jane Addams. Look closely at the huge photograph on the wall and you will see a unique panoramic shot of the city shortly after the Chicago Fire of 1871. The rubble is still smoking. The photo makes jaws drop.

The same is true of many other images Phillips has on the walls: people riding the Ferris wheel at the World's Columbian Exposition of 1893; Buffalo Bill Cody firing a rifle; Jesse James on horseback; Walter Jacobson as a Cubs batboy; prefire photos of the city's downtown; Civil War veterans and Abraham Lincoln; nineteenth-century immigrants.

Most of his collection sits in file cabinets in his West Loop space (not open to the public), more than a hundred thousand images, about half of them of Chicago and Illinois.

"Dave is a really nice and amazing guy," says Tim Samuelson, the cultural historian for the Chicago Department of Cultural Affairs. "It's like he has this bottomless well of material. All you have to ask is, 'Do you have . . . ?' and he'll come up with whatever you are looking for—and usually more."

Phillips is also a printer, a camera expert, and an inventor. His place is filled with hand-built and reconditioned machines for processing photos and rebuilt aerial spy cameras capable of creating stunning panoramic views, such as one he showed us of Wrigley Field at dusk. He took the photo.

"I've had a bypass and two hips replaced," he said. "I'm just ready to shoot again."

He is also ready to part with his collection. The price is six million dollars, about half of that for the Illinois and Chicago shots. Though we don't have that kind of dough, Osgood and I think it's an amazing bargain.

NOVEMBER 13, 2005

KEEPING PACE WITH MUSTANGS

ONE IS MORE LIKELY these days, it seems, to see kids playing soccer than playing tackle football, and so when Osgood and I were cruising east on Seventy-ninth Street near Western Avenue and spotted a pack of padded and helmeted kids doing jumping jacks in a field of grass, it was almost as if we had been transported back in time.

"Jumping jacks," Osgood said. "Who does jumping jacks anymore?"

A good question. And the answer? Dozens of young men, members of the St. Rita football team, the Mustangs, doing that very thing and doing some old-fashioned stretching exercises and wind sprints.

It was part of a familiar rite: the late-summer football practice. Let the mere fans remember crisp fall days; for anyone who played high school ball, such pleasant memories coexist with those of dehydration, the season's first banged knee and bloody nose, the first jarring hit that made your knees buckle and your head hurt.

I played, and in the early 1970s I ventured down to watch St. Rita play more than one game, for the team of that era featured a much-touted halfback named Billy Marek, who, in only three carries, convinced me that my abilities were far below what I had foolishly imagined them to be. At the time, St. Rita played its games in a stadium at Sixty-third Street and Claremont Avenue. In 1990 the school moved its campus and its games south, taking over what had been the Quigley Preparatory Seminary South.

A few parents were sitting on the small bleachers there, watching practice. To the west, the stadium was empty. There are more than a few old-timers who will tell you that the new Pat Cronin Field, named for a former coach, lacks the "magic" of the old one, but that didn't matter to the youngsters sweating and straining and grunting through practice.

The Mustangs play in the competitive Catholic Metro Blue conference. During the preseason practice, as Osgood successfully invented his version of a helmet cam, some parents expressed optimism about the coming season. Two weeks later the team won its first game against Collins. The score was 52–0, an example, some might tell you, of the benefits of jumping jacks.

SEPTEMBER 24, 2000

BOO'S SOUL KITCHEN

THERE IS A FELLOW called Big Man who is a regular at Boo's Soul Food Café, 10936 South Vincennes Avenue, and who often blames Boo for making him go off his doctor-ordered diet. Other customers accuse her of making their waistlines expand. As if on cue, one such man walked in the door of this extremely cozy and friendly café and said to a stranger, "Look what she's done to me." He patted his ample stomach, laughed, and ordered meat loaf, mashed potatoes with gravy, green beans, and peach cobbler—"always that peach cobbler."

It was lunchtime and most of the dozen or so tables in the brightly lit rectangular dining room were occupied. One of those eating was Boo herself, otherwise known as Willetta Tatum, who told us, "The name Boo comes from my childhood. It's what my mama called me. She died two years ago, just before I opened this place, and I decided to honor her memory."

Tatum opened Boo's on a "prayer and a dream" in a space next to a car wash that had already been an unhappy home over the years to four or five failed restaurants. A native Chicagoan, she learned to cook from her mother. Before opening Boo's she ran the cafeteria at the old Chicago Board of Education headquarters.

"I always wanted to start my own restaurant, and business here was good from the start," she says. "But knowing how to cook doesn't mean you know anything about running a place."

She has learned quickly. Customers are so happy with the restaurant that they bring Boo gifts such as stuffed animals, which she proudly displays.

Boo's serves great food. On any given day, diners can choose one of three entrées from a list that includes pot roast, baked ham, smothered pork chops, chicken and dumplings, chitterlings, ribs, and catfish. They come with two side dishes. And always that peach cobbler. Most meals will cost you a couple of bucks less than ten dollars.

Boo's husband, Jackie Tatum, has remained relatively thin and says, "I knew she was a good cook, but it's been great to see so many other people really enjoy her food. Some days we run out of food way before closing time." So popular has Boo's become, especially on Sundays, that many people are telling her that she needs to expand. Though she has dreams of one day opening another location, she wants this place to stay the way it is. "I love to keep it small and homey," she says. "We put a little bit of home here 'cause we're never home."

NOVEMBER 19, 2000

TAKING IT TO THE STREETS

"OKAY, WHERE TO?" asked Osgood.

"Anywhere we want," I answered.

We started walking aimlessly and soon found ourselves on the fifth floor of a building in the Loop talking to Mayor Richard M. Daley, who was telling us, "You really can't look at the city as fifty separate areas. What happens on one side of the street affects the other side. It doesn't matter what the ward is. Look at the plans for [planned development along] the river. That will have an impact on the Twenty-third, Twelfth, Eleventh, Forty-third, and other wards."

The man knows his wards and his city. Nearly every day he is in a car, and he is always eyeballing Chicago. At the sight of an abandoned building, a bedraggled park, a broken streetlight, a pothole, or some other urban blemish, he will call one of the city commissioners or department heads and demand, often in very pointed fashion, a quick solution. He remembers first driving the city as a child with his father. "He used to have to go to a lot of wakes," he says.

Whatever one may think about Daley, there is no denying his passion for this place. He has just returned from the opening of a handsome new apartment complex called Roseland Ridge in a downtrodden area of the Ninth Ward.

"I know there are problems in the city and many people are struggling just to survive," says the mayor. "This is still a city of neighborhoods, more so than places like New York or London, and people deserve to be proud of where they live, of their neighborhood's identity."

We thank the mayor for his time and leave City Hall. On the sidewalk, struck with the realization that we are free to travel in any direction we want, we decided to head south. We wanted to explore those new apartments in Roseland and anything else that might catch our eye.

DECEMBER 24, 2000

IN THE 2300 BLOCK of South Leavitt Street, Osgood and I found another fading wall sign. Most such signs surprise us, but this one was evocative. The *Chicago Daily News* was a newspaper that informed Chicagoans for 104 years before ceasing publication on March 4, 1978. It said good-bye with the jaunty headline "So Long, Chicago."

I used to work for the *Daily News*, as did my father before me and as did some of my colleagues at the *Tribune*. Each day we walk through a lobby where quotations are carved into the walls. Many, but not all, concern journalism, sentiments such as this from the playwright Arthur Miller: "A good newspaper, I suppose, is a nation talking to itself."

WRITING ON THE WALL

Not on the walls, understandably, are some of the nasty things that people have said and continue to say about this business. Nowhere, for instance, is this sentiment, courtesy of the late mayor Richard J. Daley: "A newspaper is the lowest thing there is."

We in the business are always hearing criticism of what we do, hearing that readership is down, that papers lack the immediacy and visceral punch of television, that one day newspapers as we know them will no longer exist, having been replaced by some sort of digital digest. Who knows? Many of you learned to get along without the *Daily News*, and many manage to get through each day without touching a newspaper. But for some a daily newspaper remains, even if people don't always realize it, what I like to think of as a daily miracle, an essential commodity.

At a South Side bus stop one recent morning, I watched as a young man tried to choose between those relatively new twenty-five-cent papers, *RedEye* and *Red Streak*. Each featured full-page cover photos of Madonna and Britney Spears locking lips, not exactly what I think of as news. But the young man stared back and forth at the covers, back and forth. Finally he shrugged, fished some coins out of his pocket, and did something that warmed at least one heart. He bought them both.

SEPTEMBER 21, 2003

A TASTE OF COTTON CANDY

COTTON CANDY HAS A STRANGE TASTE, one difficult to describe. We asked some kids recently, and they said "like sugar," "like weird bubble gum," and "like straw that was dipped in sugar," among other responses. None were much interested in talking. They were more interested in eating the cotton candy and otherwise enjoying that distinctive neighborhood event known as a carnival.

There are pleasures to be had in the relatively sterile playground that is Great America, and there's some fun available at Navy Pier, but nothing can match the rough-and-tumble treats and intimacy of the neighborhood carnival. Osgood and I look for them every summer, and it seemed to us that there were fewer of them this year. We finally discovered one, and a good one it was: the Rogers Park Carnival, put on by the United Church of Rogers Park over four late-July days and nights in the 6900 block of North Ashland Boulevard.

The best thing about urban carnivals is that they come at you (especially if you are a kid) unexpectedly, erupting in what seems like an instant in various places like magical cities, all sparkling and ready to go. It is a bit of magic, really: what one day is a vacant lot is transformed, the next night, into a forest of neon and sound and movement. There is a bit of danger, too, depending on the amount of rust clinging to the rides. And knowing the impermanent nature of these events gives visitors an urgency—you can see it in their excited eyes—to take it all in, in one exhausting gulp, before it all fades away.

The Rogers Park Carnival has been held for more than a decade, and most of those who were there had been there before. Others, discovering it as they might a secret city garden, will try to cling, over the fall and winter and spring, to the memories of where it was and when. And the strangely pleasing taste of cotton candy.

AUGUST 25, 2002

NO PLACE LIKE HOME

FORMER WBBM-TV ANCHOR Linda MacLennan remembers the Zhou brothers, and so do I, because one day in 1986 MacLennan and I interviewed them live on TV from Taste of Chicago, an annual summer gathering in Grant Park during which hundreds of thousands of people stuff themselves with food from dozens of Chicago restaurants. The brothers, artists visiting Chicago from their native China for a small gallery exhibition, spoke no English at the time and thus became part of one of the most awkward segments in local TV history.

"I almost strangled the producer who booked them," says MacLennan, now happily away from TV, living in the suburbs as a wife, an accomplished photographer, and a mother to three children. "But they were such nice guys and good sports."

They still are. Shan Zuo Zhou and Da Huang Zhou (pronounced "Joe") moved to Chicago a few months after the 1986 interview. They came with two suitcases and thirty dollars in their pockets, and they found a place to live in Bridgeport. They have been expanding it ever since into what is now a vast complex that serves as their home and studio. There's also a lovely sculpture garden and more than enough space for the students who come from around the world to study at the brothers' art academy every summer. Part of their complex was once a restaurant where the mayor worked as a busboy when he was young, says Shan Zuo (on the right in Osgood's photo and five years older than his brother).

Chicago provided the perfect creative environment. "For many years here we did not have demands on us," says Da Huang. "We could work because we were not so much in the local spotlight." But their work soon began getting international acclaim and exhibitions at prestigious galleries and museums. Only recently has Chicago taken notice.

Asked if they remembered that long-ago interview, the brothers smiled, and Da Huang said, "The lady Linda was very nice."

The pair travel often but, surprisingly, like being here in December.

"We enjoy the lights and the decorations and the way the city looks," says Da Huang.

"We stay here because this is our home," says Shan Zuo.

NOVEMBER 28, 2004

SET 'EM UP

LINCOLN SQUARE LANES, 4874 North Lincoln Avenue, has been in the bowling biz for more than sixty years. It has only twelve lanes, a spacious cocktail lounge, a pool table, a small balcony area with lockers that hold the paraphernalia of league bowlers, and prices so reasonable they seem frozen from some previous decade. It has that sort of vanishing neighborhood feel that can make neighbors of strangers. "Good roll," a teenage boy says to the forty-eight-year-old stranger on an adjacent lane after watching him make a four-pin spare.

On this Sunday afternoon, eight of the lanes are in use by a father-daughter duo; a group of beer-drinking men on two lanes; three teenagers; a pair of families—one with a grandmother who bowls with her own ball—on two lanes; a couple on a date; a lone man in a T-shirt. Later a group of college-age kids will take over three lanes for a birthday bowling party.

It is the kind of crowd one doesn't see much in this increasingly stick-with-your-own-kind city: a mix of both sexes, all ages, many nationalities and professions, white collar and blue. But it has always been a people's game. When introduced to colonial America, bowling was played outdoors and was immediately condemned by Puritans, who believed it promoted gambling and laziness. The game was then called ninepin bowls, or skittles, and was banned in some of the thirteen colonies. Eventually, they say, some shrewd Connecticut settlers added a pin and bowling moved indoors as restaurant and tavern owners realized they could attract customers by offering the amusement. In 1840 a British visitor observed, "Of all species of [participant] sports, bowling was the national one in America."

Bowling was at its most popular in the 1960s, after the invention of the automatic pinsetter made large facilities financially practical (and forced a lot of kids and some winos who worked as pin boys into new careers). New and elegant centers were built in the suburbs, but eventually the boom went bust. Many big centers closed and others struggled. The industry responded by marketing such attractions as Cosmic Bowling, which adds loud music, dim lights, and even fog machines to the mix, and offering innovations such as bumper bowling.

These new wrinkles have put off some purists, one of whom told me, "I like bowling 'cause it's the only sport where the arena of competition provides players with ashtrays." But they have kept the game alive and allow such places as Lincoln Square Lanes to continue to thrive; to function, on a subtle level, as social focal points for neighborhoods and work colleagues; and to provide a home, an arena, to those athletes who remain ever allergic to running and sweating.

APRIL 9, 2000

A CAT AND MOUSE STORY

AN INTERESTING GUY, this fellow G. K. Wuori staring at a mouse.

On October 13 he saw in *Chicago Tribune Magazine* the story Osgood and I did about a fifteen-foot-tall cat that sits on the corner of Roosevelt Road and Waller Avenue, the cat named Carl. We told readers about the Big Kitty and thought, for most people, that would be that.

But in Sycamore, Wuori logged on to his computer and typed this e-mail, which he then sent to the magazine: "It's clear to me that the come-hither look on your giant cat's face is due to its looking out toward Sycamore and a mouse that even a cat that size can only dream of. As is true of your cat, I can't find anyone who knows the real story behind the mouse, but it would be a real hoot if the sculptor of each was one and the same person, and clearly one with a sense of humor."

The nine-foot-tall mouse sits near the corner of Main Street and North Avenue near the Kishwaukee River. Wuori speculates that "it's in what I think was at one time a church camp, because there are a few abandoned camplike buildings" nearby. Wuori, a DeKalb native who moved back to this area from Maine four years ago, has never seen any sort of function on the grounds. "Nor," he says, "does Sycamore have any kind of iconic mouse in its history. The mouse just sits there. Sometimes it inspires in me a kind of Stephen King–ish reverie, but nothing's come of that yet."

Wuori is a man given to reverie, as befitting his profession. He's a writer. His first novel, *An American Outrage,* was published in 2000. A *Tribune* reviewer called it "magical." So it pains us a bit to have to inform Wuori that the Big Kitty in Chicago is staring southeast and not west toward Sycamore.

But does it really matter?

It's nice to imagine that all things are possible, that there is magic in the air.

DECEMBER 22, 2002

KIDS STUFF

A LITTLE GIRL WE KNOW was screaming at her parents one day to be taken to the American Girl store on Chicago Avenue, threatening to "jump out the window if you don't take me."

Osgood and I still love toys, though we don't often throw tantrums to get them. But liking toys was one of the many reasons why, driving west on Belmont Avenue one recent afternoon, we found ourselves pleasantly lost for a while inside Uncle Fun.

This is a toy store to encounter the unexpected or the long forgotten. It is filled with hundreds of items, most priced nicely between fifty cents and ten dollars and some of them icons of vanished youth. Osgood and I have been visiting the store, on and off, for a decade or so, and here are some of the things I remember buying there: a snow globe containing Elvis, a *Baywatch* doll, dozens of bracelets, a handful of small rubber frogs, a boomerang, and some troll dolls with brightly colored hair. Though I recall that the troll dolls were given to six-year-old girls attending a birthday party, I have no recollection of what I did with the other things. For all I know, the *Baywatch* doll was a bachelor party present or may have wound up as part of some beach sand sculpture. But what happened to the gifts isn't really the point, is it?

The point is that they were a joy to find. Shopping at Uncle Fun is a gloriously goofy experience, and there you are likely to encounter many more adults than kids, such as owner Ted Frankel (from left), clerk Brett Nevue, and manager Andy Needham in Osgood's photo. Indeed, there one day was famous local restaurateur Demetri Alexander, who told us, "I first came in here about eight years ago looking for Elvis pictures for a gag gift, and since then I'm in here all the time. No matter what you're looking for—stuff from *The Jetsons, The Partridge Family*—the place will bring you back to a more whimsical place. I don't want to sound like a shrink, but this place lets you get in touch with your inner child. And the people who work there are so neat and, well, fun."

Alexander and his friend spent two hours in the store. "He had never been there before, and he loved it. I finally had to drag him out," Alexander said.

We don't know if the little girl who was screaming got her trip to American Girl, but I like to think she might have equally enjoyed a trip to Uncle Fun and perhaps might have found some pleasure—even some future memories—in a rubber frog, or a troll doll with purple hair.

MARCH 25, 2001

JAZZ AND GUNS

DAVID BLOOM HAS AN IDEA.

This is not an unusual occurrence. Bloom is filled with ideas and is never loath to express or explore them. He carries around a little recording gizmo into which he speaks his thoughts, observations, and ideas. He has for more than a year been making a documentary about the meaning of "soul" and has interviewed on videotape dozens of people, including Studs Terkel, Oscar Brown Jr., and some kids at the University of Chicago Lab School, his alma mater.

He is the younger of two sons of Sophie and the late Benjamin Bloom. She taught reading in public schools. He was a University of Chicago professor whose research and books have influenced generations of educators worldwide and formed the foundation of the Head Start program.

David fell in love with music early and hard, drawn to blues and jazz. In the early 1970s, after returning to Chicago from studying at the Berklee College of Music in Boston, Bloom was playing nightclubs and supplementing his modest income by teaching music. It was during this time that he got what would prove to be one of his best ideas.

"I was thinking that the connection in the classroom was more intense and rewarding than what I was experiencing on the stages of most local clubs," he says.

He scraped together enough dough to open the Bloom School of Jazz on the sixth floor of the Pakula Building at 218 South Wabash Avenue. The school is thriving as it moves into its fourth decade.

So is Bloom. He is a publisher; his Fire and Form series now includes five instructional books. He is a book reviewer for the *Tribune;* he wrote about Studs Terkel's 1957 *Giants of Jazz,* handsomely reissued in 2002, and later wrote about former *Tribune* jazz critic Larry Kart's collection *Jazz in Search of Itself.*

Bloom's latest idea is this: free music lessons in exchange for handguns. "I have already had discussions with the Chicago Police Department and hope to be able to launch the program by spring," he says.

There are, of course, many details that need to be worked out before that can happen. "And I want to make it clear to people that learning to play is not easy," he says. "But I guarantee if the people listen to me and practice, I could have them up on a stage in six months. Think about it: a battle of the bands instead of a battle of the gangs."

Don't need to think about it. It's a great idea.

FEBRUARY 6, 2005

OF BAR STOOLS AND BARBERSHOPS

VAN BUREN STREET IS NAMED in honor of the eighth president of the United States and, Osgood and I will strenuously argue, the most interesting street in the Loop. In *Chi Town,* author Norbert Blei devotes a chapter to the street, asking, "But who sings of old Van Buren, groveling there like a lost hymn under the El tracks, holding the line of the Loop's south end?" Well, he does, writing about the businesses and people and feel of the street a couple of decades ago, including a joint called the Rialto Tap, with a window sign that read WE SERVE ALCOHOLICS.

The street has changed since then, but it still makes for a colorful walk. Keep your eyes and ears open. You will be rewarded. You might fall in love with Frank's Barber Shop, which sits on street level in the glorious Monadnock Building at 56 West Van Buren. The black-and-white tile floor, the efficiency and pleasantness of the barbers, the loquaciousness of the clientele (many of them lawyers), all conspire to make a visitor feel like part of the real Chicago.

People don't hang around barbershops the way they used to. Hell, people don't go to barbershops the way they used to. They go to stylists, salons.

Oh, what they're missing.

At Frank's you can hear about a fellow named Alphonso "Pete" White, who died in 1990. He shined shoes at Frank's, and among his steadiest customers was George Halas, who would walk over from the Chicago Bears offices when they were on Jackson Boulevard. Halas liked White so much that in his will he bequeathed him a lifetime sideline pass to Bears games.

You might also learn that as a young man Frank Yonder, who started the shop, was a member of the Guido-Yonder gang, a notorious group of burglars who concentrated their efforts on the North Shore. He was pinched, did his time, and went straight. "He was the best boss," an employee said of Yonder, who died last year.

And those are just two real Chicago stories from a real Chicago street.

NOVEMBER 30, 2003

IN 1873 A COIN WAS FLIPPED to determine the name of a small town near the Illinois-Indiana border. Heads and it would have been State Line. Tails and it was Hammond, after businessman George H. Hammond, who, with some pals, had opened one of the largest meatpacking plants in the world and shortly afterward opened the ominously named State Line Slaughter House.

And so, here it is, its population now in the neighborhood of 80,000, down from a peak of about 130,000 in the early 1960s. Of course, as has happened to small cities here and everywhere, the opening of large shopping malls helped give the downtown section of town a bruised and beaten look.

The first time we fell in love with Hammond—a city known to most Chicagoans for the delicacies at Phil Smidt's and the double-down opportunities at a nearby casino—was when we

HOPE IN HAMMOND

discovered an amazing mural a few years ago. It is fifty-six feet long and eight feet high, painted in 1965 by soon-to-be-famous-and-rich LeRoy Neiman. It is a lively and colorful backdrop to the tellers at the Mercantile National Bank. It is titled *Summertime Along Indiana Dunes*. Say what you will about Neiman—and serious critics lambaste him for his commercialism and flamboyant personality—but this mural is beautiful, one of a handful he created before hitting the big time.

"Customers are always commenting about it," says Rhonda Cavazos, who works in the bank's marketing department. "It really adds something special to the place, especially in the dead of winter. Every day it makes me smile."

And when is the last time you heard the word "smile" associated with "bank"?

The Mercantile National Bank and its branches have been run for three generations by the same family. Christopher Morrow, the current board chairman, says his grandfather, Jack Murray, was in New York in the mid-1960s and one night in a tavern he struck up a conversation with a young artist who turned out to be Neiman.

"One thing led to another," Morrow says, "and that artist came here and painted the mural. He even put my mother in the painting."

Thirty years ago Neiman made a deal with a New York restaurant to hang ten of his prints. "I agreed that they could have the prints as long as I eat complimentary," Neiman recently told a New York reporter.

Morrow happily reports that his grandfather obviously made a better deal. Neiman has never walked into the bank demanding cash, though Morrow would like to have him come back

to Hammond to see how well his mural has held up and how it continues to warm the usually icy world of finance.

Osgood often drops into Hammond, cameras at the ready, while on his way to and from getaway weekends in Michigan. And that is how we discovered the LaSalle Hotel. Built as a granary in 1908, it was, at five stories, big for its time and place. During the 1920s it was converted into the Hotel Meade and was used to store bootleg booze and house gangsters during Prohibition.

That's owner Louis Karubas in Osgood's photo, manning the cage that is the hotel's front desk and where he sits seven days a week for twelve hours, beginning at 6:00 A.M. Born and raised on a farm in northwest Nebraska, he worked for a time for the State of Indiana before buying the hotel in 1970. It was in bad shape, and he made many trips to Chicago to buy furniture and other items at liquidation sales for such bygone hotels as the Pearson.

"When I started to rebuild this place, it was important to me to leave the old-fashioned touches, to keep the hotel's character," he says.

Most of the seventy rooms are occupied by permanent residents, a few of whom commute to Chicago. He says he runs a place that is "strict and safe."

Karubas has seen Hammond change a lot in his quarter century there, living through the city's ups and downs. He believes himself to be "the last businessperson to have stuck it out this long." He says he will happily show visitors around his hotel and steer them to some other interesting spots. He has hope for Hammond. That's why he stays.

"It's simple, really," he says. "I like this city."

MARCH 20, 2005

118

KEEPING THE FAITH

ON THE 5800 BLOCK of West Division Street are seven storefronts. Four are empty but three are home to places of worship: the True Love Mission, the One Way Church of God in Christ, and the Christian Progressive Achievement Center. Across the street is the One Church in Christ Baptist and nearby is the Holy Trinity Church of God in Christ.

The latter has a sign in its window: A CHURCH WITH A MESSAGE FOR THIS MESS-AGE. Forty-three-year-old Robert Taymore was walking down the street and was asked what he thought the sign meant. "What do you think it means?" he said. "Just look around, man. There are a lot of messed-up lives around here."

Osgood was shooting pictures and talking to a man named Herman Cunningham. He said he was sixty years old, owns three trucks, and had recently injured himself in a fall. He is old enough to have seen the neighborhood in better times and young enough to dream that better times might find it again. "There was a movie theater right here and stores," he said. "Now you can't buy an onion or nothing around here. You don't have no restaurants for coffee."

Cunningham said he would like to buy the seven storefronts and turn them into stores. He has nothing against religion but said, "The churches are only open but one day a week." Actually, some of them are open more often: Tuesday night Bible study classes, Wednesday prayers, and Friday night services. They would, presumably, find new homes if Cunningham realizes his ambitions for the area.

The Austin neighborhood is a long way from the glitter and prosperity of other sides of town. But the close gathering of houses of prayer there didn't surprise us. Just look in the phone book and you will find hundreds of churches and other places of worship in areas of the city and suburbs you've never heard of and would never think of visiting. But Osgood and I often stop in such places. If our experience is any indication, in all of these venues you will be greeted by a smile and perhaps an outstretched hand. You will be made to feel welcome.

It's good to do that every once in a while, just drop in. It is a fine way to remind yourself that the world may not be as crazy as it often seems to be, at least in matters of religious choice. Sooner than later, though, you'll again be reminded that this remains a "mess-age" and that every day, amid prayers for peace and happiness (and, yes, we suppose, winning lotto numbers), people scream at, beat, bomb, maim, and kill each other in the name of their God.

DECEMBER 10, 2000

ADVENTURES IN THE SKIN TRADE

IN THE SUBURB OF STONE PARK, Scores, which bills itself as the nation's premier gentlemen's club, recently opened its first club outside Manhattan at the intersection of Lake Street and Mannheim Road. This sort of place, though not uncommon in large cities and small towns across America, offends some. The notion of naked and seminaked women dancing for the visual pleasure of men makes people mad.

"We don't want such a spot here," one local resident, a woman in her midthirties, told us.

Dana Montana's heard that before. She originally opened the club that is now Scores under a different name some fifteen years ago.

"I'll bet that same woman complaining has been up to the Sugar Shack and didn't find anything wrong with that," says Montana.

The Sugar Shack, on a country road just outside Lake Geneva, is more than twenty-five years old and has hosted tens of thousands of women who have come there to see nearly naked men dance. Montana was an ex–Playboy bunny and the single mother of three (a boy who later danced at the Sugar Shack and two girls who've never performed; all three now work with her) when she opened that place.

"This is not about sex," said one Scores dancer. "It is about the appreciation of beauty. We are not in the sex trade. There's no fooling around. Dana makes sure of that. We dance here because we want to dance here. We dance, period."

There's no denying that America's still pretty uptight about sex. For all who find gentlemen's clubs abhorrent, there's an equal number who (perhaps not so publicly) appreciate the clubs.

"This is a beautiful room with beautiful women," said a forty-nine-year-old man from Houston in town for a convention. "I am married, happily. My wife knows I visit gentlemen's clubs. She knows what I know: there are a lot more dangerous activities a man on the road can get into than just looking at lovely people."

NOVEMBER 9, 2003

LIFE AT A BUCK A BAG

THE DECEMBER WIND is blowing and biting, and on the spot where the westbound exit ramp of the Eisenhower Expressway meets Laramie Avenue stands a man wearing a tattered snowsuit, a hooded sweatshirt, a cap, heavy boots, a Bears jacket, gloves, and, curiously, a big smile.

"I got good days and I got bad," says Thomas Gaither. "Winter's coming now, but I'll be here. If it gets too cold for my body, I'll give it up, but it ain't ever got too cold for me."

Gaither is a member of a small army that works the ramps of the area's expressways. He is a veteran, having held this spot for twenty years selling bags of peanuts, small plastic spray bottles of air freshener, and, when he can buy them inexpensively, teddy bears or incense. He started his street corner career when he lived nearby, on Congress Parkway, and now that he lives in Blue Island he commutes to work by means of a battered brown station wagon.

"This corner's helped me raise two children," he says, speaking with pride of his nineteen- and fourteen-year-old sons. "I remember when my baby was born. I was standing right here when my auntie ran over and said, 'Get off this corner and get to the hospital. You just had a baby.'"

Gaither works this West Side spot five or seven days a week, from 8:00 A.M. until about 4:00 P.M. On a good day he sells sixty or seventy bags of nuts.

"But you can't expect a good day every day," he says. "Things used to be better. There were days when I'd sell out. Those were good days."

A few regular customers make daily purchases, but often Gaither will go hours without selling one one-dollar bag of peanuts.

"You gotta be patient," he says, in what makes a fine philosophy of life. "And no matter how that wind blows, you gotta keep smiling."

JANUARY 9, 2000

ROUGH ROAD

A FEW WEEKS AGO, Michigan Avenue came ablaze with lights. The street was filled with Disney characters, the air alive with music and fireworks, the sidewalks thick with people, and the store windows jammed with goodies. The Magnificent Mile Lights Festival, sponsored in large part by the *Tribune,* is all in the name of holiday spirit. The Tribune Tower and other Michigan Avenue buildings were suitably bedecked in seasonal greenery and lights.

Now, Osgood and I are not among those who carp about the Christmas season's increasingly early start. We don't care if it's Christmas every day. But we do get a little irritated by the pervasive commercialism of it all, the spend-spend-spend pressures.

The sign in Osgood's photo is a long way from Michigan Avenue. We found it a few miles from Du Quoin.

One meaning of the word "hardscrabble" is "producing or earning only a very small amount," but it has come to mean downtrodden or just plain poor. It was first used two hundred years ago by Lewis and Clark in their journals to describe barren land. It caught on quickly and in a decade attached itself to the area of Chicago now known as Bridgeport.

Hardscrabble Road has a few well-tended homes, but it made us think about how many more byways could qualify as hardscrabble roads rather than magnificent miles. And we hope this will give us some perspective when we decide how to spend our money this holiday season.

It also reminds us of a story.

In 1854 Ulysses S. Grant retired from the army and tried to settle into civilian life, moving near his wife's family in St. Louis and buying a farm. On his eighty acres, he built by himself a home made of hewn logs and large timbers. He called this place Hardscrabble, and he raised potatoes and sold firewood. He wasn't very good at it, and his lot was made worse by a financial panic in 1857. All but ruined, the future Civil War hero and president of the United States was forced to pawn his watch. He used the money to buy Christmas presents for his family.

DECEMBER 12, 2004

INNOCENCE OF THE COWS

THERE IS A GENERATION of local kids who will now be able to grow up unencumbered by thoughts or dreams of evil cows.

For more than 125 years, children had to live with the knowledge (or at least a legend so ingrained that it passed for truth) that a cow was responsible for one of the major disasters in Chicago history. We all learned at an early age that on the hot Sunday night of October 8, 1871, when Mrs. Catherine O'Leary went out to the barn behind her house on DeKoven Street to get some milk from her cow, the cow kicked over a lantern, which set fire to nearby hay. That started the Great Chicago Fire, which leveled much of the city and killed as many as three hundred people.

But in 1997, thanks in part to the work of Richard F. Bales, a lawyer by trade and a historian by passion, the cow and Mrs. O'Leary beat their bad rap. Bales's digging was what compelled Alderman Ed Burke of the Fourteenth Ward to state at a meeting of the Chicago City Council Committee on Police and Fire, "Mrs. Kate O'Leary and her cow are innocent." The real culprit appears to have been a character named Daniel "Peg Leg" Sullivan.

Bales's research is in book form: *The Great Chicago Fire and the Myth of Mrs. O'Leary's Cow*. And in what some may view as mere coincidence and others may see as justice finally served, the city's most prominent cows have a brand-new home. Lincoln Park Zoo's new Farm-in-the-Zoo opened last month. A six-million-dollar renovation has given it a snazzy and roomier look and added all manner of new exhibits and activities.

One recent visitor, eleven-year-old Hannah Wolf, was especially taken with an exhibit that simulates weather conditions on farms. She also had an interesting observation: "One person came in and was showing a cow to her little baby and said, 'Look, honey, a horse!'" As silly as that may be, it is also an indication of how far we urban dwellers are removed from farm life. Cows (as well as pigs, sheep, and goats) are now seen by little children as exotic animals.

Osgood and I visited with cows named Tasha, Diamond, and Lillia at the new farm and found them very likable. They mugged for the camera (that's a smiling Tasha in the photo) and transfixed the wide-eyed little kids who came by—kids who can now grow up thinking of cows as important and altogether innocent creatures.

OCTOBER 6, 2002

THE FIXERS

A MALE COLLEAGUE who claims to have more than fifty pairs of shoes might do well to introduce himself and his closet to Michael and Marian Moretti. They run Michael's Shoe Repair, a small shop at 900 Green Bay Road in Winnetka, a ninety-minutes-each-way trip from their home in Kenosha.

Michael is a third-generation shoe person. When his grandfather Luca came here from Italy, he worked as a handyman until he was joined by his family. He and his son Michael Sr. then opened their first shoe repair shop in Mount Prospect and later moved themselves and the business to Highwood.

"Over the years, my father started selling shoes, and the repair business became kind of an afterthought," says Michael Jr. "The old equipment moved to the back of the store and eventually into my grandfather's basement."

But when Michael Jr. began selling shoes with his father, he became intrigued by the old repair equipment. "I was always interested in mechanical stuff, and there was just something about these old machines," he says. "I started to repair shoes as well as sell them. Finally, my father said I had to make a choice: sell 'em or fix 'em."

The fix was in, so to speak, and Michael and Marian opened their Winnetka shop in 1995. Business has been very good, which might seem surprising, since we are living in an increasingly disposable age.

"I have clients from the city to Lake Forest, and I repair a couple of hundred pairs of shoes a week," says Michael, whose shop likewise mends purses and luggage. "I think it has to do with the comfort factor. The older we get, we don't find comfort as easily as we did, and when we find it, we want to keep it. That and the time factor. Who has time to shop for new shoes? Who even likes to shop?"

Married for thirty years, Michael and Marian are at their shop Tuesdays through Saturdays. They have three grown children, none of them in the family business.

"But you never know," says Michael. "When I was their age, I didn't think I'd be doing what I'm doing now. They call this a dying art, but they are only half right. This is not dying, but it really is an art."

NOVEMBER 30, 2003

A FEW DOZEN PEOPLE gathered under a tent at a place called Montrose Point in Lincoln Park. Many of these people, never having been to this particular spot before, were thrilled by the view of the city skyline, perhaps the most beautiful offered from anywhere on the North Side.

They had assembled to dedicate a section of park dotted with trees that were newly planted in honor of columnist Mike Royko, who died in April 1997. The location, near a harbor filled with boats, was more than appropriate, because Royko loved boats and the park. And, as his brother Robert said, observing a nearby refreshment stand, Mike "liked a decent hot dog."

The brains and energy behind this memorial was Royko's sister, Eleanor Royko-Cronin, who works for the Chicago Park District and is the coordinator of its two-year-old Green Deed Tree Dedication Program, which allows people to have trees planted in the city's more than five hundred parks.

ROCKY AT ROYKO'S GROVE

The dozen or so trees in Royko's Grove had been purchased by Royko's friends, family, and colleagues. There was one from Iron Mike's Grille, the restaurant owned in part by Mike Ditka, who was a big Royko fan; he carries an old Royko column in his wallet. Studs Terkel and his wife, Ida, bought two trees. Sam Sianis and his family purchased a skyline honey locust, for Royko was more than a good customer at Sianis's Billy Goat Tavern. He was Sam's best friend.

Small tags were affixed to the trees, and people wandered about finding theirs. On a sunny afternoon a few days later, the wind whipped ferociously, making it unseasonably cold. A woman and her white poodle jogged. A couple sat on the rocks that line the shore. A lonely boat, an exotic-looking Chinese junk sort of boat, bounced on the waves. And a solitary man, a large man named Bonacio Kimbrough, was doing calisthenics.

"I like the environment," he said, adding that he has lived in Chicago all his life and had driven up to this place today from his home in the Marquette Park neighborhood. "When I used to live near the zoo, I used to ride my bike up here. I just love the whole skyline."

When asked about his unusual first name, he said, "Yes, sir, it is different, but everybody calls me Rocky."

During the summers, Rocky works building and setting up carnival rides. In the winters he does what he can.

"I just made forty," he said proudly. "I love my city and the truth of everybody in it."

Did he know Royko?

"I've heard that name," he said. "He has some nice new trees here."

NOVEMBER 29, 2000

132

HOT DOG FEVER

HOT DOG FEVER BEGINS, unofficially of course, on opening day of baseball season. An organization called the National Hot Dog and Sausage Council ranks ballparks according to hot dog consumption. In 2004 Wrigley came in third with 1.47 million, behind Dodger Stadium and Coors Field. We did not know that. Come to think of it, there is much about hot dogs Osgood and I don't know. "And maybe don't want to know," he says.

But we have stopped in more than our share of hot dog emporiums while driving around (the spot in Osgood's photo is at the intersection of Gross Point Road, Central Street, and Crawford Avenue in Evanston). We understand why people like hot dogs.

But it is hard to relate to Takeru Kobayashi. He is from Japan, and last year on the Fourth of July at Coney Island, he ingested (you just can't call what he does eating) fifty-three hot dogs in twelve minutes, breaking a dubious world record. Learning of this hot-dog-eating record, I was irresistibly drawn to an outfit called the International Federation of Competitive Eating. Its list of records is, in a word, nauseating.

The IFOCE lists records for eating more than seventy different foods, from conventional eating contest fare such as doughnuts, pizza, and chicken wings to reindeer sausage, rice balls, and Spam. Some records amaze. A man named Eric Booker ate forty-nine glazed doughnuts in eight minutes. And what to make of a thirty-eight-year-old, 409-pound man named Cookie Jarvis, who has the record for cannoli, chicken fingers, chicken-fried steak, corned beef and cabbage, dumplings, ham and potatoes, ice cream, pasta, pork ribs, french fries, and sweet corn?

For his hot dog efforts, the 131-pound (give or take) Kobayashi got a trophy, a championship belt, and a year's supply of hot dogs, whatever a year's supply might be for such a hungry fellow.

The rest of us pay as we eat. And between bites at a baseball game this year you might want to share some information with your fellow hot dog eaters. Though there are a number of stories about the origin of the name "hot dog," we like the one that starts on an April afternoon in 1900 outside the old Polo Grounds in New York. Baseball fans were offered skinny sausages from vendors shouting, "Get your red-hot dachshund sausages!" A cartoonist sketched a drawing of barking sausages for the next day's paper. Unable to spell "dachshund"—yes, I had to look it up—he came up with "hot dog."

APRIL 10, 2005

ART OF THE STATE

NO DOUBT MANY OF YOU know the number of home runs Ernie Banks hit in his career, but do any of you know the name of the artist laureate of Illinois? Were you aware that such a character existed? Culture usually takes a backseat to baseball, so it doesn't bother the artist laureate that you don't know her name. "Oh, who would have time to be bothered by that?" she says.

Her name is Kay Smith, the state's artist laureate since 1994. She's there, in Osgood's artful photo, reflected in glass that covers one of her beautiful watercolors. It is titled *Kay Smith's Homestead, Vandalia, Illinois.* The people in it are Smith's grandparents George Washington Willet and his wife, Albina. Smith grew up in the house.

"The first painting I ever did was in kindergarten," she says, a gentle laugh sneaking out. "A polka-dot giraffe."

Her work matured, and eventually she made her way to Chicago and studies at the School of the Art Institute, a marriage, a daughter, work as a professional illustrator, and, starting in 1971, her consuming life's work. The American Legacy Collection now numbers more than 250 watercolors and sketches, a vivid and imaginative trek through five hundred years of American history. Though many of her other works sell for thousands of dollars, Smith refuses to break up the collection, hoping that it might one day find a permanent (and necessarily large) home.

"The dream? For it to be seen in its entirety," she says.

Now in her eighties, she still paints, though not every day, and does some teaching. She is ever eager to talk about art and history.

Becoming Illinois's artist laureate "really did change my career," she says. "It gave me authority and opportunities. I was so nervous at the presentation that I could not rise from my seat."

That ceremony took place in Springfield, where eighty-four of her paintings, what she calls the heart of the American Legacy Collection, went on display today at the executive mansion. Springfield is only about two hundred miles southwest of Chicago and not far at all from the pretty little town of Vandalia.

APRIL 17, 2005

A STREET-SMART FELLOW

MADISON STREET FAMOUSLY INTERSECTS State Street. Though no longer the busiest corner in the world, as civic boosters claimed for decades, it remains the city's most essential corner, the baseline from which the city's streets begin their orderly numerical march east, west, north, and south thanks to a man you have probably never heard of: Edward Paul Brennan.

Born in Chicago in 1866, he first went to work in his father's grocery store. From 1893 to 1929, he was a bill collector and building superintendent for the Lyon and Healy music company.

Brennan lived in a city nearly impossible to navigate. For various reasons, primarily the annexation of villages such as Lake View and Hyde Park, the streets of Chicago were a confounding puzzle. There were, for instance, thirteen streets named for George Washington. There were seven Fortieth Streets, nine Sheridan Streets, and ten Oak Streets.

With no formal training but an agile mind, Brennan devised a plan to fix this mess. He first made his ideas public in a 1901 letter published in the *Chicago Record-Herald,* and a cousin who was an alderman presented it to the city council. Brennan suggested the city use State and Madison Streets as the dividing lines on which the numbering of streets could be based. He also suggested the odd/even numbering system and new street names, hundreds of which were adopted. One bold idea—naming streets alphabetically—never fully caught on but is manifested in the K, L, M, N, and O Streets on the city's West Side.

In July 1937 Brennan was honored with a city council resolution, and five years later, at the time of his death, it was noted that Chicago had 3,629 miles of streets with 1,370 names. Other cities that were much smaller in area than Chicago had many more street names: New York (5,003), Baltimore (3,929), and Cleveland (2,199).

That same year Chicago got another street name when a stretch of pavement between Ninety-fifth and Ninety-eighth on the Southeast Side was designated Brennan Avenue, even though Brennan lived most of his life on the North Side.

In 1958 Brennan's three daughters gave the Chicago Historical Society seven scrapbooks titled *Chicago's Street Numbering System and Nomenclature,* with thousands of newspaper articles relating to Chicago's streets that their father had cut from papers published between 1884 and 1942. One daughter, Adelaide, says, "Our father never accepted any monetary reward or political favors for himself, his family, or his friends."

Brennan made order from chaos, and wherever you're going and wherever you've been, you owe him a debt of gratitude for making the trips so smooth.

SEPTEMBER 28, 2003

WINTER WONDERLANDS

LOOK AT THOSE FACES in Osgood's photo. What do you see? Yes, a bunch of kids visiting one day at the DuSable Museum of African American History at 740 East Fifty-sixth Place. But what else? Check out the eyes of some of the kids and then ask yourself, Is it possible to see wonder?

That's what I think I see in those eyes. Osgood and I couldn't tell you exactly what has captured their interest. The DuSable Museum is filled with eye-catching exhibits. The kids could be looking at any of the more than twelve thousand pieces in the museum's collection. The point is that something wonderful is happening.

There must exist, somewhere, photos of me with an expression similar to those of these kids as I stared into the Chicago Fire diorama at the Chicago Historical Society; or looked at the stuffed gorilla Bushman encased in glass at the Field Museum or at a painting in the Art Institute (though, for some reason, art doesn't always have the same capacity for inducing wonder in youngsters as does seeing chickens hatch); or watched the stars twinkle at the Adler Planetarium or the fish swim at the Shedd Aquarium. Somewhere along the bumpy ride to adulthood I misplaced the capacity for easy wonder. It happens to all of us. We get hooked on TV or video games or phones that take pictures and distract us from simpler pleasures.

There is no doubt that many museums, or at least those with sufficient funds, recognize this trend and have remade some exhibits in flashy high-tech ways that are intended to keep us interested enough to drag our kids through the doors. And though such updating no doubt has a certain appeal for the Game Boy generation, don't lose sight of the fact that the ability to stir wonder in young eyes is still there in the simplest items in the smallest museums and historical societies.

Winter is the perfect season to revisit and reexplore one of the dozens of museums and the increasing number of historical societies in the area. You don't have to be a kid to be enriched by the experience, but it would help if you can remember what it was like being a kid. And consider yourself lucky if you see a bright yellow school bus parked in front.

NOVEMBER 21, 2004

MAKING A MARK

OSGOOD AND I DON'T SPEND a lot of time looking at license plates, but while cruising along Milwaukee Avenue one day, Osgood excitedly said, "Hey, look at that license plate!"

It read ART COP, and at the next stoplight Osgood pulled up alongside the car and we recognized the man in the passenger seat as the artist Robert Heinecken. We had featured him in a 1999 *Sidewalks* because he had painted a face on the wall of a building he shared with his wife, photographer and School of the Art Institute teacher Joyce Neimanas. Heinecken told us at that time that some neighborhood kids had splashed the building and the face with graffiti.

"At first I was mad," he said. "It was such a nuisance to clean up. But as I was doing that, I realized what they were doing is not so different from what I had done. They were just trying to make their mark."

That observation stayed with me, and I started thinking of vanity license plates as yet another way in which people try to make their mark.

Osgood convinced Heinecken and Neimanas to take the plate off their car and hold it up. Neimanas said she has had the plate for more than a decade but was reluctant to explain its meaning, and good for her. She did say that she and her husband were, after thirty years here, going to live and teach in New Mexico. This made Osgood wistful; he recalled that in the mid-1970s Neimanas was his teacher and adviser when he was on his way to a master's degree in photography. "She was really good, really hard," he said. "She was really an inspiration to me."

So Osgood and I have promised ourselves that from now on we will pay more attention to license plates. As I told him, "You just never know who's behind the wheel."

MAY 16, 2004

TITO CHACON GETS HIS HAIR CUT at Hair by Mario, a small but extraordinarily busy barbershop on West Montrose Avenue, as busy a barbershop as there is in town. Every five weeks or so, thirty-three-year-old Tito takes a bus—two buses, actually—to get there after his weekday shift as a waiter at the Billy Goat Tavern.

"I once went on a Saturday morning, and the line was down the block even before the place was open," he said.

On the night Osgood and I accompanied Tito to Mario's, we arrived to find a couple of dozen people waiting. "This is nothing," Tito said.

And so he waited, surrounded by a wildly mixed crowd: young and old, men and women, fathers and sons, and a lot of teenagers. I don't know if there is a barbershop in the United Nations building in New York, but if there is it must look and sound a lot like Mario's. I could hear a number of languages being spoken.

TITO GETS A HAIRCUT

Sal Aburumman was sitting in a chair, watching one of his three sons get a haircut. They had driven to Mario's, as they did every five weeks, from their home near Ninety-fifth Street and Western Avenue.

"Isn't that a very long way to come for a haircut?" I asked.

"Yes, it is," he said. "I could find a closer place, but it would not be the same. The drive is not so bad when you think about the history." As he kept a close eye on his son's head, being tended to by barber Eddie Issa, Aburumman said, "Many years ago when I was a boy in Jordan, Eddie's father would cut my hair."

Eddie Issa is one of seven sons of Mohammed Issa. All of them are barbers, and Eddie and his older brothers, Chris and Mario, cut hair in Chicago.

"My father taught us well," said Eddie.

Testimonials were not more than a few feet away, in the form of twelve-year-old Nestor Solis. He and his pal Frankie Guzman are regulars.

"They cut good," said Solis. "And the price is not too high."

The hairstyle favored by these young men, and by many patrons of Mario's, is called a fade. Popularized by professional athletes in the 1980s, a fade is basically a crew cut, with the sides of the head shorn to varying lengths. A full fade takes the sides down almost to bare skin.

The barbers at Mario's were lively and affable, though they barely had time for conversation. The seven full-time and two part-time barbers were constantly busy from the moment the place

144

opened at 9:00 A.M. until it closed, usually a bit after 8:00 P.M. Each averaged some 40 haircuts a day, an average of one every sixteen minutes or so, and Issa claims the official shop record of 120 haircuts in one day. "I worked extra hours that day," he said, smiling.

After more than an hour, Issa pointed Tito to a chair. But it was not for his haircut. First he would have his eyebrows plucked and shaped.

"I didn't want to do it at first, but every time I would come, I'd see all these guys, young guys, getting it done, and they look pretty good," he says. "I used to think that just women did the eyebrows, but it's very big with men now."

A woman named Kathy Michael got to work, and as she did an expression of pain crossed Tito's face. "It hurts only a little bit," he said.

The process is called threading, and it is an ancient art, a form of hair removal first practiced in India, Pakistan, and the Middle East. The threader, using a strand of sewing thread, basically lassoes out each hair with the looped end of the thread. To watch the process is to marvel at the dexterity of the threader. And those in the chairs will tell you that they prefer this to the more familiar hair removal methods of plucking, tweezing, and waxing because it is chemical free, more precise, and can remove hairs too short to be removed by wax. For men, the popularity of threading is surely generational. "I don't get it," said a sixty-two-year-old plasterer named Warren Blake, who was waiting for a haircut. "It's for the kids. It's not for me. But then I don't have no tattoos or earrings."

Tito's threading took only a few minutes; it cost five dollars. Afterward, he looked as though he'd been sobbing. And still, with a cold towel pressed against his brows, he waited. After twenty minutes or so, Issa pointed him to a chair. Tito sat down and said hi to his barber. Her name was Vivita Lejina. She is from Latvia. She has worked at Mario's for four years and has worked on Tito's head for eight months. It took about twenty minutes to give Tito a fresh look. He favors a relatively tall two-inch or so top and a semifade for the sides.

"Do I look good," he said in a manner that made it difficult to determine whether it was a statement or question.

His chair was immediately filled, and more than a dozen people were still waiting. A rainstorm of hair showered the floor's black-and-white square tiles. Words peppered the din. "On any day, you will hear thirteen different languages being spoken in here," said barber Alex Santana, working on head 37 of what would be a forty-two-haircut day.

JUNE 18, 2000

146

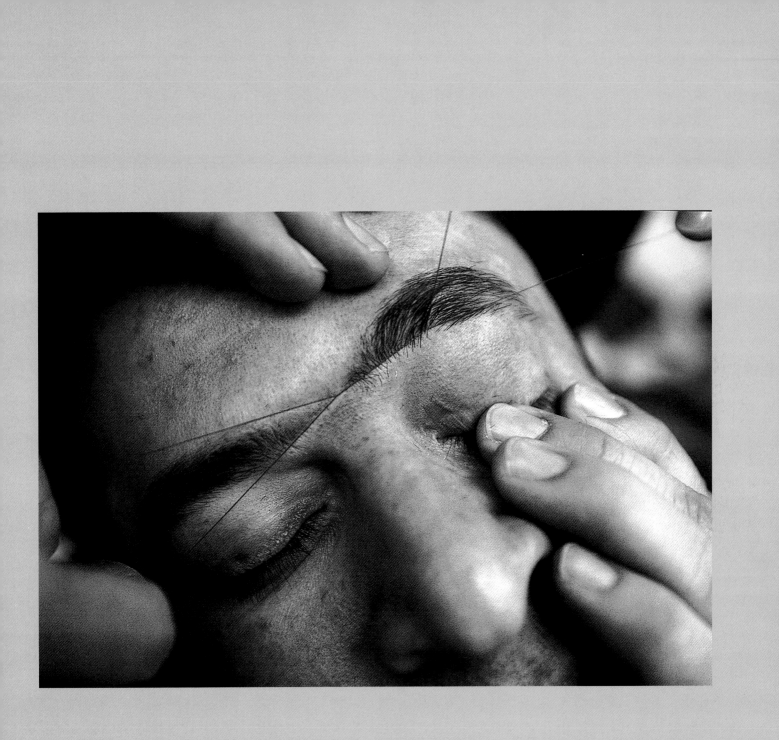

THE ROADSIDE GALLERY

IT WAS A SAD DAY when the Magikist sign went down. The red-lipped urban icon, located where the northbound Kennedy Expressway meets the Montrose Avenue exit, vanished late in 2003. Its demise was chronicled by my colleague Eric Zorn. He wrote about it, quoting architect and preservationist Jonathan Fine: "[People] will feel a true sadness to learn the lips are gone, like an old friend from the neighborhood has died."

Ever since, Osgood and I have been keeping our eyes off the road.

"There's another one," Osgood will say, and our eyes will move toward whatever billboard sits on the side of the road, up in the air.

We are newly nuts for billboards, whether touting some morning radio show, used-car dealership, casino experience, or new housing development. The Magikist sign was one of three that used to dot the city (the others were at Eighty-fifth Street and the Dan Ryan Expressway and at Cicero Avenue and the Eisenhower Expressway). It was less of a billboard than a flashy neon construction, but billboards in all their manifestations still do quite nicely, if you'll take a look.

That's how we found Wally Przewoznik, on a ladder near Belden Street and Pulaski Road, removing a bank ad that he was going to replace with one for Clear Channel, the communications giant. Watching him peel away the goateed man's face reminded us of the days when billboards were painted by hand, thus creating what was, in essence, a nationwide roadside art gallery.

Computers changed all that, with their ability to mass-produce giant images. What also changed the "gallery" was the Highway Beautification Act of 1965. It dulled the roads, limiting billboards to commercial or industrial areas and requiring states to set limits on size, lighting, and spacing of the billboards.

But it's still a healthy business. According to the Outdoor Advertising Association of America, five and a half billion dollars were spent in 2003 on outdoor ads. That figure includes money spent on advertising on the sides of buses and elsewhere, but the bulk (62 percent) was spent on billboards. There are an estimated four hundred thousand of them.

JULY 18, 2004

A THRIVING FIVE-AND-TEN

IF YOU ARE STANDING ON THE CORNER of Milwaukee and Campbell Avenues, just north of Armitage Avenue, you will notice another of those "Now who the hell is this?" honorary street signs that dot the city. This one is particularly wordy: ARTHUR "JULES 5 & 10" GARTZMAN WAY. It was installed in 2000 to honor the man who ran the store just up the street, the Jules Five-and-Ten, where you can still buy parakeets and finches (two for eighteen dollars) and almost everything else known to man, woman, and child, though few, if any, of the items are priced at a nickel or a dime.

Gartzman took over the store in 1958 from his father, who had opened it in 1947. It is now owned by the smiling fellow in Osgood's photo, Modesto Serna.

When the store first opened, the five-and-ten business was dominated by the Woolworth chain of some five thousand stores in big cities and small towns. Woolworth's most prominent presence in Chicago was on Michigan Avenue and took up the entire block between Erie and Huron Streets.

On the outside wall of Jules Five-and-Ten is a sign: THE STORE THAT HAS IT ALL. When the weather cooperates, some of what the store has is displayed on the sidewalk: shoes, luggage, clothes, birdcages, baby strollers, and tricycles.

Inside, it's a place in which to get pleasantly lost as you wander down the tightly packed aisles. And while shoppers in the stores along Michigan Avenue can "enjoy" piped-in Enya, the noise inside the five-and-ten is real. Birds serenade customers, because a considerable portion of the place is a pet store containing a variety of creatures, from birds to rabbits to snakes to rainbow lizards to puppies, such as the cute little Yorkie-Maltese mix Serna is cradling in the photo.

Some may think of this place as a relic, but it is a vibrant part of its neighborhood. A Polish woman told us she has been shopping here for forty-one years. A man said that he was making his first visit, having arrived days before from Mexico.

The Woolworth chain went out of business in 1997, but wandering around Jules Five-and-Ten it's easy to recall the familiar Woolworth slogan—"Everybody's Store"—and think that this lively survivor is just that.

MAY 23, 2004

A REFUGEE'S LASTING LEGACY

SHERIDAN ROAD BEGINS at Diversey Parkway before snaking its way north all the way to the Wisconsin border. On the northwest corner of the Diversey-Sheridan intersection you will find two similar sculptures, one on each side of the entrance to the Stone Medical Center. Titled *Brotherhood,* they were installed decades ago when the building served as headquarters of the Amalgamated Meat Cutters and Butcher Workmen.

They are two sets of kneeling bronze figures, now weathered to a green patina: two-man, two-woman groups meant to represent the working people of Europe, Asia, Africa, and North America, their arms intertwined to suggest inseparable entities. The statues sit about three feet above the sidewalk, making it virtually impossible for people to see the messages on all four sides of their bases. On the Sheridan statue are the words BROTHERHOOD, LIBERTY, TOLERANCE, EQUALITY. The other displays FRIENDSHIP, JUSTICE, KNOWLEDGE, PEACE IN UNITY. Nowhere is the artist identified.

His name is Egon Weiner; he fled his native Vienna in 1938, shortly before his mother was taken by the Nazis. He would never see her again. He made his way to Chicago, where he eventually became an instructor at the School of the Art Institute from 1945 to 1971. He was eighty-one when he died here in 1987.

But his work lives on in *Brotherhood;* in the thirty-three-foot-high *The Pillar of Fire* at 558 West DeKoven Street, near the spot where the Chicago Fire began; in *The Christ* on the North Park College campus; in *Ecce Homo* at the Augustana Lutheran Church at 5500 South Woodlawn Avenue; and in a fourteen-foot statue in front of St. Paul Lutheran Church at Tenth Avenue and Lake Street in Melrose Park.

A 1975 collection of his lectures, *Art and Human Emotions,* begins with a perfect thought for a particular season: "When in springtime, the flowers grow again after a lonesome, dreary winter, we are all happy, and I am even happier because I know my mother loved flowers so much . . . Whenever I see flowers, I meet my mother again."

MAY 11, 2003

A COLD DAY IN PARADISE

IT WAS ONE OF THOSE DAYS that did everything but scream, "It's winter, you idiots, go inside." The windshield wipers of Osgood's car had been fighting a losing battle with the first sleet storm of the season, and when we got out of the car to explore a sixty-acre patch of Chicago known as Sherman Park, we did feel, frankly, like idiots.

A few grammar school kids strolled through the park, but they were not interested in nature but rather warmth, hurriedly making their way home or to the Chicago Public Library branch that sits at the park's southeast corner.

"You two guys crazy," said one of the boys to us.

Extending south and west from the corner of Racine Avenue and Fifty-second Street, the park is a place of remarkable physical beauty, an area of willows and wildlife, tall trees and flowing prairie grass, and more than a few birch trees, some of them gently scarred by the carved initials of long-ago visitors, perhaps some of them lovers still loving. The park's principal feature is a lagoon stocked with catfish each year but also containing bluegill, largemouth bass, carp, and other species. The lagoon surrounds a large island with tennis courts and ball fields, which is accessible by four bridges of various architectural styles.

The park was designed by Frederick Law Olmsted, the landscaping genius most famous for his design of Central Park in New York and Jackson and Washington Parks in Chicago. It is named in honor of James B. Sherman, a mostly forgotten fellow who lived from 1825 to 1902 and was once known as the Father of the Stockyards. He was also a park commissioner and the father-in-law of the visionary planner-architect Daniel Burnham, who designed the Prairie-style field house that still stands at the park's northern edge.

The neighborhood that surrounds the park is one tragically marked by violence and crime. Until a few years ago, the park was an unofficial meeting ground for members of a street gang. But its combination of beauty and charm and natural pleasures makes it hard to believe that it could not have a calming effect on even the most savage souls. There are more than five hundred parks in this city. This may be the loveliest of them all.

DECEMBER 17, 2000

154

THE DEATH OF BIG KITTY

IT IS ONE OF THE SADDEST THINGS Osgood and I have seen in some time. We had just been driving around as usual when we decided to visit our friend Big Kitty. We first told you about the big kitty in October. We told you that it was fifteen feet tall with a blue necklace from which hung a green shamrock pendant bearing the name Carl. The big kitty was an object of curiosity and speculation in the neighborhood. No one Osgood and I talked to could remember when it first appeared or what it was doing there. There were many theories, none of them very sensible or sane. I had written that "some people have pelted the cat with rocks, mistakenly believing that it was put there by the FBI and has 'secret cameras' inside." At the end of the column, after explaining that Big Kitty had been placed on the corner by the city's largest film, video, TV, and commercial production facility after having served in a television show, I asked, "Hey, folks, now that you know the truth, how about leaving the big kitty alone?" Osgood and I, hoping for the best, found the worst: Big Kitty beaten to death. Now, there are many more serious problems in the city in these times than the destruction of a foam rubber statue, but somehow the death of Big Kitty seems sadly symbolic of a world in which idiots run onto baseball fields to attack innocent people, deface the property of others, abuse wives and children. The death of Big Kitty reminds me that the line between mischief and cruelty remains frighteningly thin.

MAY 4, 2003

THE SANDS OF TIME

AMONG THE MOST PLEASANT childhood memories are of lazy days spent at the beach. But there is no beach in Bolingbrook. "And that's why the whole week before we came here, the kids were really excited. 'When are we going? When are we going?'" said Karen Brewster, who lives in the southwest suburb.

She was lying on the sand at Foster Avenue Beach, keeping an eye on her five young children while lazily chatting with her friend Jeanette Dattilo, who was watching her three kids.

"We all packed into the van to get here," said Brewster. "It was jammed."

In addition to the women and their eight children, the van also carried Eugene Gatewood, a friend who was "here for moral support," and a little boy visiting from Iowa.

Foster Avenue Beach being a considerable distance from Bolingbrook, I asked, as if I couldn't guess, what had brought them here.

"I grew up just a few blocks from here," said Brewster. And Dattilo added, "My father lived nearby."

The beaches of our childhood get under our skin for keeps. Changing beaches is almost as serious a personal alteration as changing your name.

"A beach gets in your blood," said Brewster. "But as kids, living so close, going to the beach was no big deal."

It was a big deal for the nine kids she had driven here—and would drive here throughout the summer at least twice a month.

"It is," Brewster said, "the cheapest form of entertainment."

Cheap but priceless. The kids built sand castles. They wandered to the water's edge and giggled when the waves hit their tiny toes. They chased gulls and kicked sand. The mothers and Gatewood talked about the things grown-ups will talk about, as if unaware of the magic they were giving to these nine little kids, the magic they will surely remember.

JULY 2, 2000

UNEASY NEIGHBORS

THE STREET WAS QUIET in the middle of the afternoon. Kids were not yet home from school. Parents were at work. Older women and, less frequently, older men were strolling down the sidewalk—on their way someplace perhaps, the store maybe, but looking blissfully possessed of all the time in the world. In a few homes, cats could be seen lounging on windowsills, catching sun.

It could have been any of a dozen Chicago neighborhoods, for that is where to find simple pleasures in the middle of the day and out of the way—removed from commercial strips and busy thoroughfares. That is where the real Chicago lives.

Look at the houses in Osgood's photograph: old and new, side by side. This is how the city most frequently changes: block by block, house by house. It is a wonderfully intimate change, less jarring to the eye than a new skyscraper jutting into the air or a former mattress factory converted to lofts.

Still, these small alterations can make some people uneasy. We are territorial creatures, and the sight of strangers in our midst can be jarring. But it can also be encouraging, a sign of healthy revitalization and not mere gentrification. Indeed, many developers are stuffing their pockets by building ticky-tacky town houses. But most of the people moving into the new and the renovated are doing so for a fine reason: they want to. They want to be your neighbors.

The dwellings in the photo are some of many old/new groupings on display. It has happened before and it will happen again, though some of the city's neighborhoods have years to go before catching the eye of urban pioneers.

In 1909 the Association of Commerce published an official guidebook that characterized the city's neighborhoods as "little cities within the metropolis, each speaking its own language, clinging to its hereditary customs, and in large part governing itself." That is no longer true for many neighborhoods. Some of the neighborhoods we remember from our youth—Little Italy, parts of Rogers Park—have been transformed so powerfully by new stores and new buildings they no longer are able to tell us we were once there, were once a part of them.

It is easy to get wistful for the city that used to be—for the corner candy store, the fruit peddler, the parking anytime. But most have learned to accept that such a place no longer exists. And so we try strenuously to become comfortable with the city's new faces, if not always its facades. We move from place to place hoping that we'll like the new neighbors and that they'll like us.

OCTOBER 18, 1998

THE OLDEST LIBRARY

AFTER SOME WELL-DESERVED rest and relaxation with her husband, attorney Phil Corboy, Mary Dempsey was back in the book biz after serving for eight months as the interim head of the city's Department of Procurement Services. She has returned to the job that she adored for—can it really be that long?—more than eleven years. As Chicago Public Library commissioner, she has overseen multimillion-dollar investments that have resulted in the opening of modern new branches and the renovations of old ones, the introduction of computers and other technological updates, and the creation of the One Book, One Chicago program.

Many of us have all but abandoned libraries for the Internet, given up card catalogs for Google, books for blogs. But there are wonders in all of the more than eighty libraries in the city system, and Osgood and I happily direct you to one of its jewels, the Blackstone Library, at 4904 South Lake Park Avenue. It is the city's first branch library and its oldest, built in 1904 with money donated by Isabella Norton Blackstone in honor of her late husband, Timothy Beach Blackstone, a railroad executive and the first president of the Union Stockyards, who had died four years earlier.

The building, impressive as any in the city, was the work of architect Solon S. Beman, who designed much of Pullman, the Fine Arts Building on Michigan Avenue, a few Hyde Park homes, and a couple of buildings for the World's Columbian Exposition of 1893. He created a beautiful library modeled on the Erechtheum, a temple on the Acropolis in Athens. It has solid bronze doors; a central rotunda supported by eight marble columns and graced with four large murals by O. D. Grover depicting Literature, Science, Art, and Labor; and a main reading room whose high ceiling features a leaded-glass skylight.

No wonder branch manager Anne Keough is proud of the building. The place would be worth seeing even if it were empty. But it's not. There are more than thirty-six thousand books on hand. Go check one out.

OCTOBER 16, 2005

RICK TUTTLE HAS BEEN IN LOVE with books for as long as he can remember, and for the last decade that love has manifested itself in the most compelling and, indeed, loving ways.

Tuttle is a man of many trades: painter, writer, carpenter, and graphic designer. You might have seen his work, if not his name. He designed, for instance, the handsome logo for Southport Records. He also transforms books into visual works of art.

"It all started because I couldn't afford to collect really fine editions of books," Tuttle says. "I would buy these crummy old editions, with tattered covers and broken spines, and I just one day was compelled to mend them."

Not just mend but playfully, artfully embellish. His first creation was a leather binding for Jack Kerouac's *On the Road,* with a tire tread worked into its cover. Next was a first edition of

HAPPY ENDINGS

Gabriel Garcia Marquez's *One Hundred Years of Solitude,* for which he built a walnut slipcase; then *Tarzan of the Apes* inside a log, *Christ in Concrete* in concrete. Tuttle says he comes up with ideas for his art/books while reading, which he does voraciously and eclectically. His work is always surprising, always inventive.

Seeing Tuttle's work gives one a new appreciation of the power of literature to inspire creativity. The ways in which he has been moved by words would make any author proud.

Tuttle is married to the legendarily lively actress-artist-teacher Donna Blue Lachman. They are in love. No one who has ever seen them together could dispute it. Near one another, they seem to glow.

But to observe Tuttle inside his B Books store in the increasingly artsy Michigan town of Three Oaks is to realize that he can become drunk with affection for inanimate things as well, as many seductively line the shelves of his shop.

Tuttle and Lachman gave up their Pilsen loft to become permanent Michigan residents, settling into what had been their summer home. Lachman, the founder of the bygone Blue Rider Theatre Company (1984–99), is head of the drama department at La Lumiere, a LaPorte, Indiana, boarding school with an international student body.

"I am so happy here," she says. "Jealous? No, not at all. I love that Rick is in love with books, and he has me reading more than I ever did before. He's never been happier. And what woman doesn't want her man to be happy?"

DECEMBER 30, 2001

CREATURES OF THE BEACH

THE SKYSCRAPERS THAT so impressively line the lakefront have started throwing shadows earlier across the sand and concrete of the city's beaches. Summer is wearing thin. But still in bright sunlight, a nicely tanned man named Jeff Gates sits on the concrete near Division Street. On his shoulder is a bird. It is a four-year-old umbrella cockatoo named Quincy, and he is here three days a week, traveling from the apartment he shares with Gates near Sheridan Road and Foster Avenue. They skate here, the bird riding on Gates's shoulder.

Gates is a pianist and graphic artist who prefers this stretch of beach for "the obvious reason," which is not so obvious, since he motions in the direction of both a lovely bikini-clad woman and a breathtaking skyline view.

"At first Quincy was spooked," says Gates. "Until last summer he was an indoor bird. He had never had blue sky above him. He's very comfortable. People come up to us constantly. He pulls a nice crowd. Maybe it's a little ostentatious, but people are enamored of it."

Quincy cocks his head as a breeze ruffles his feathers. He could fly away if he were of a mind—and if he weren't tethered to Gates by a leash.

"He loves it here, so much that he gets a little funny in winter," says Gates. "He seems to be depressed in March and April."

As Gates is talking, another creature emerges from the passageway that runs under the streaming traffic of the Outer Drive. It is a small dog, a three-year-old toy poodle almost as small as Quincy. The dog is Dinky, and her owner is Amy O'Keefe. They live, with O'Keefe's husband, in a nearby high-rise. They are here three or four afternoons a week, if it's not too hot.

"We adopted the dog after it had spent its first year or so being terribly abused," says O'Keefe. "Shortly after we got her, she suffered a spontaneous rupture of a disc. She had an operation, but it didn't work. One option was to put the dog down, but she was still so vibrant, we just couldn't."

So O'Keefe contacted an outfit called K-9 Carts, based in Big Sky, Montana. It supplied the little contraption that allows Dinky to playfully scamper from sunbather to sunbather.

"Some people think I'm torturing the dog, but most are very friendly and very interested," says O'Keefe. "And she loves the attention."

Nearby a man rises from his towel and begins to do push-ups. A woman stands and slathers herself with baby oil. The shadows continue to lengthen.

AUGUST 23, 1998

A TOOTHPICK *TITANIC*

THERE ARE SOME PEOPLE you need to keep tabs on, and Wayne Kusy is one of them. I first heard about him five years ago when, as an editor at the *Tribune,* I got a phone call. "There's this wild guy in town," said a young writer named Jeff Favre. "He makes these huge boats out of toothpicks. I want to write a story about him."

"Go ahead," I said, and in a few weeks he turned in a fine and fascinating story.

A few Saturdays ago, there was a good-bye dinner for Favre, who's going out to California to find fame and fortune as a screenwriter. He said that he had talked to Kusy and that he was still making things out of toothpicks, so I decided to check in on him.

"I'm doing great," Kusy said.

We talked about the *Titanic* he finished in 1985, a 75,000-toothpick affair nine feet, eight inches in length. It is in a Los Angeles museum. We talked about the *Lusitania* he built in 1994. It's a sixteen-foot, 194,000-toothpick giant. It's in a Baltimore museum. He recently finished a handsome version (eight feet, 16,000 toothpicks) of the clipper ship *Cutty Sark* and is working on his biggest project, the *Queen Mary,* which he estimates, when finished in a year, will measure twenty-five feet (1 million toothpicks, give or take). He works on the ship evenings in two- or three-hour shifts. His method involves using pliers to crush the toothpicks into more pliable forms.

He works days as a marketing assistant. He is in a band called Heavy Mental. He is thirty-eight years old. He lives in East Rogers Park. He now has his own Web site. He traces his current passion to playing with Legos as a kid and to a grammar school project that called for creating art from items such as Popsicle sticks. He built his first ship, with a modest three thousand toothpicks, when he was in sixth grade.

"Ships fascinated me," he says. "It was the size. They are really buildings that float. I wanted to know, How do they do that?"

Though there might be some who deem his creations mere novelties, Celeste Sotola is not among them. When she displayed Kusy's *Titanic* at her Enid Oklahoma Gallery in River North in 1994, she said, "Wayne is in the truest sense an artist because he's a loner, he doesn't follow anyone else's lead, and the amount of time he spends on his art is a real symbol of his dedication."

APRIL 19, 1999

WELL TRAVELED

MORE THAN FIFTY YEARS AGO, a pregnant Chicago woman, for reasons psychological and spiritual but altogether impossible to detail, decided that her first child should be born in Santa Fe, New Mexico. The mother was a white woman of British descent. The baby's father was a black man whose ancestors came here as slaves from Nigeria. A few weeks ago, their daughter, who was born in Santa Fe and whose name is Laurel Stradford, was happily showing us photos of her parents and saying, "Perhaps I was just born to travel, to be kind of a gypsy."

The marriage did not last, but the daughter has thrived. She now owns a store called What the Traveler Saw at 1452 East Fifty-third Street in Hyde Park. This is where she was raised and has lived most of her life. She attended the University of Chicago and Columbia College, studying various arts and earning bachelor's and master's degrees. She made art, taught school for a time, and continued to help, as she had for years, at the clothing store her mother owned in the Harper Court shopping center. She became an image consultant for some of the store's customers and such places as the DuSable Museum's gift store. In the wake of an Operation Push–led boycott of Revlon products in 1986, she boldly offered her services to that company. To her great surprise she was hired for an executive position. She worked for the company for thirteen years, many of those as export manager based in her large Hyde Park home. Later, living in London, she traveled throughout Africa, Asia, and Europe for the company. "I learned to be fearless when I travel," she says.

But she eventually tired of "the loneliness of corporate life." Returning to Chicago, she worked as director of special events for Chicago State University, began selling art out of her house, and helped organize the shops in the outdoor marketplace near the Garfield Park Conservatory. She operates her two-year-old shop on a philosophy long ago imparted by her now eighty-seven-year-old mother: "A store should have the personality of the person who owns it."

What the Traveler Saw lives up to its promise of "wonders from around the world," but it also carries the work of artist Steve Clay, Stradford's former husband, who remains a close friend. She also stocks other local artists' work as well as candles, jewelry, purses, lamps, razors in the shape of dolphins, decorative boxes, vases, and many other interesting and beautiful things. Among the most intriguing are volumes of Stradford's ongoing autobiography, slender five-dollar volumes that combine her gifts as photographer, collagist, and writer. She tells of her ancestors, her parents, her sister, and herself in what she calls "a document of sights, thoughts, and feelings of the life traveler."

JUNE 5, 2005

A PATCH OF PEACE

THERE IS LITTLE FOOT TRAFFIC along the 800 block of South Oakley Boulevard, no matter the season. There are businesses to the west, a school to the north, and some baseball diamonds to the east, but on most days you could go hours without seeing a soul strolling down the block.

So only a few people ever stumble upon the Vietnam Survivors Memorial, at 815 South Oakley Boulevard. It is a 50-by-125-foot grassy plot, a glory of handmade serenity. Its focal point is toward the back: ten cast-iron pillars painted a deep red that stand in a circle around a mosaic map of Vietnam embedded in concrete. The park also features flagpoles, lights, gargoyles, a stone path, and benches.

Bill Lavicka, who was in Vietnam in the late 1960s as an officer with the Navy Seabee construction crews and who returned to Chicago to make a successful career as a builder and preservationist, is the person who created this park. He did so a year after being inspired by the two million people who showed up here for the 1986 Vietnam veterans parade that went a long way—if not all the way—to healing the war's wounds. He created a foundation and donated a lot he owned. He convinced the state-run Illinois Medical District Commission, which owns extensive property in the area, to do likewise with an adjoining lot.

The neighborhood has changed considerably in the eighteen years since the park opened. The lots were once worth about five thousand dollars each, but a nearby lot of similar size recently sold for two hundred thousand dollars. Lavicka is worried that the medical district might be forced to sell its plot, and he is lobbying strenuously to keep that from happening.

We talked with him when he was at the memorial a few weeks ago with his son Kelsey, a captain in the U.S. Army, home on leave from Iraq. A week later we came back and found a man sitting alone. He wasn't much for conversation but did say he served in Vietnam, was a lifelong Chicagoan, and visited the memorial every time his business, whatever that is, took him to the neighborhood.

"This place takes me to a place of peace," he said, and that's just where we left it, hoping he could stay forever.

JANUARY 12, 2003

IN A DAY'S WORK

THIS IS NOT YET a dot-com world, though it must often seem that way as we are flooded with stories of dot-com millionaires and of the wonders of using e-this and e-that for our daily needs, as we become increasingly tied to computers for work and play.

Driving around the city, it has been easy to observe that Web pages and e-shopping have not yet touched in any profound way the lives of many people who work here. The two men smiling in the picture are named Earl Norris and Robert "T-Bird" Mitchell, and they work at a place called Thomas Auto Parts on South Halsted Street, one of the hundreds of small businesses that exist in the area without the benefit of Bill Gates. They are among many thousands who spend each day working with their hands. I am sure it is possible to order tires and other auto parts via the Internet, but many residents of the Englewood neighborhood avail themselves of the palpable goods at Thomas Auto Parts and of the human expertise of Norris and Mitchell.

A few weeks ago I met a man picking through a garbage can in an alley near State and Division Streets. He did not want to talk, did not want to tell me his name, did not want to even tell me what he was doing, though it was obvious from the items he had in a large bag that he was looking for things he might later sell: pieces of metal and cans. However hard his life may be, there was a certain pride in the way he brushed me off, saying, "Leave me alone now. I am not bothering you or anybody that I know of. I am just out here trying to get by. Now get away and let me do my work."

I left him alone but within a couple of blocks realized, not for the first time but for the first time in a long time, how simple and low-tech so many lives remain. Of course the city is no longer the place described in Carl Sandburg's famous poetic vision "Chicago"—"Flinging magnetic curses amid the toil of piling job on job, here is a tall bold slugger set vivid against the little soft cities"—but in certain corners that spirit lives on.

I do not begrudge all those people enamored of, getting wealthy from, or beholden to personal computers. But meeting people like Norris and Mitchell—or the waitress at the corner diner, the guy bagging groceries, the cop on a horse, the construction worker hauling bricks—should remind us that there is an honesty and dignity in what too many of us might now deem "old-fashioned" work as we make our way through the increasingly icy world of American commerce.

NOVEMBER 26, 2000

LIFE AND DEATH ON THE RIVER

OSGOOD AND I CROSSED the Chicago River. Thousands do every day, most without realizing that it has three branches and is some fifty miles in length and twenty-one feet at its deepest. It has one island—Goose Island—and something in the neighborhood of twenty-five species of fish. There are two golf courses hugging its shores and two cemeteries. And—oh my, when did this happen?—all these new restaurants and cafés.

"What a wonderful river," said Helen Menendez, who was sitting and staring at the water, not even noticing the nearby plaque that overlooks the river, on Wacker Drive just east of LaSalle Street.

This plaque is a small reminder of the morning of July 24, 1915, a day that began so happily, even though there was a steady rain. To the river they came that day, twenty-five hundred people, most of them employees of Western Electric and their families, dressed for a company picnic to take place in Michigan City, Indiana. They had boarded the excursion steamer *Eastland* by 7:00 A.M., many seeking shelter from the rain on lower decks. At 7:25 the top-heavy boat began to sway. It broke loose from its moorings and swiftly settled on its side.

"It was like one big scream and everything was quiet," one survivor told a reporter at the time. "I was like a monkey in a barrel and headed for the side of the boat . . . for the river."

More than eight hundred people died—terrible deaths, trapped or trampled belowdecks; drowned, one writer said, like kittens in a sack. Most were young workers from Berwyn and Cicero. But there also were twenty-one entire families—gone. One of those who didn't die was a young man who overslept and missed the boat. His name was George Halas, and he went on to . . . live.

Few are left who remember the terror and tragedy of the *Eastland* disaster. The dead are long buried and the stories get dusty—lost. But the river, of course, flows on. It is now thick with boats trumpeting the architectural joys of the city, the history of the town. More people than ever are enjoying the river, on it or above it, staring into its waters and feeling glad to be alive.

JULY 25, 1999

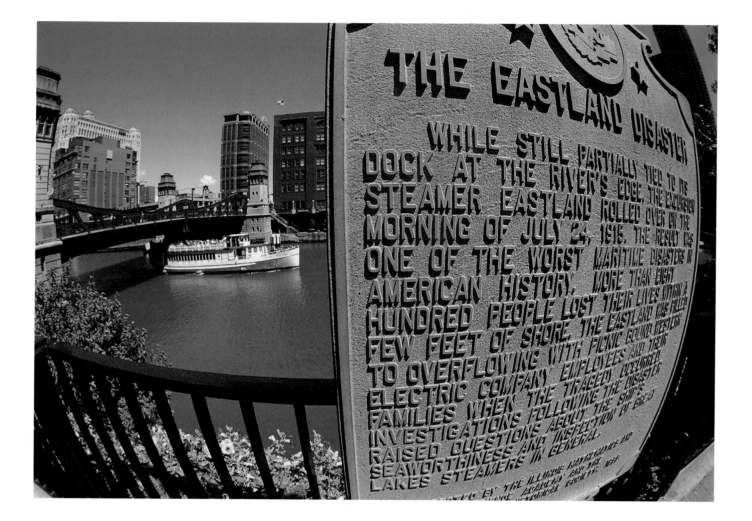

HAM AND *FROMAGE*

IF YOU ARE LOOKING to run into some of the nice and intelligent people who work for North-western University Press, not to mention others who attend classes or teach on Northwestern's Evanston campus, it would be a good idea to drop into Al's Deli around lunchtime. Actually, there are many good reasons to visit this small and special place at 914 Noyes Street.

Al's has been a popular and relatively secret spot since it was opened in 1949 by Al Pottinger. He had been a cook in the navy during World War II and later worked for a time at a Jewel store before setting out on his own, launching Al's as a grocery store that sold sandwiches. Over the years the place has evolved into one of the best restaurants we've ever visited.

Al's son Bob, the white-haired man in Osgood's photo, joined the family business after graduating from college and working on George McGovern's unsuccessful 1972 presidential campaign. "My father had to go in for cataract surgery, and he said, 'As long as you're a bum, you might as well run the store while I recuperate for two weeks.' That two weeks has turned into forty-two years."

His brother John, behind him in the photo, started at the deli in 1975, and together they have created a place of high-quality food with a distinctly French twist. "We are both Franco-philes and pick up a lot of ideas when we are in France," says Bob. He is going back later this month and has a ticket for an opera gala on New Year's Eve. "It's black tie, so I have purchased my first tuxedo."

On his last visit to France he noticed a long line of students waiting to get into a tiny bakery. Discovering the reason, a multiseed baguette, he returned here with a sackful and worked with his pals at Red Hen Bakery on Milwaukee Avenue to re-create the special baguette for the deli.

"We are always adding items to the menu, experimenting. And we must be doing something right," says Bob. "And not to brag, but I consider myself to be the best soup maker in America."

None of the regulars would argue, filling the place six days a week (closed Wednesdays) from 11:00 A.M. to 4:00 P.M. and ordering soup, sandwiches, and, as one of the editors from nearby Northwestern University Press enthusiastically attests, "the greatest cookies on the planet."

DECEMBER 18, 2005

THE WIND, AS IT FREQUENTLY DOES, whipped around the plaza that surrounds the IBM Building, which sits near the river between Wabash Avenue and State Street. This is one of the city's windiest spots. In the winter it is necessary for the building to erect rails of ropes so that people can traverse the space without getting blown over. "$%!#," said a man in the plaza as his hat was whipped off his head by the wind and tossed across State Street. "They don't call this the Windy City for nothing."

But it is not because of the wind.

In some quarters it is fairly common knowledge that the Windy City moniker has to do not with the weather but rather with bombast. The specific origin is still in shadows. When asked about the phrase, one *Tribune* reporter said, "It was coined to describe, I think, some speeches

ANY WAY THE WIND BLOWS

that were made by the old Mayor Daley. Or was it Jane Byrne? Maybe someone a long time ago. Could it have been Big Bill Thompson?"

Though there are references to the phrase in newspapers from the 1850s, what really seems to have permanently affixed the nickname to Chicago were events that took place decades later. This is the story we like. During the several years' competition to host the World's Columbian Exposition that would mark the four hundredth anniversary of Columbus's discovery of America, editor Charles Dana in his *New York Sun*, commenting on the promises our upstart city was making, wrote, "Don't pay any attention to the nonsensical claims of that windy city. Its people could not build a world's fair even if they won it." We did, of course, build that world's fair, outbidding older and richer cities for it, even if it opened a year after originally intended.

But we have never been able to shake that Windy City tag, even though fourteen U.S. cities have higher average wind speeds than Chicago's 10.4 mph. Boston's is higher, with a 12.5 mph average. Honolulu is higher, with an 11.3 mph average. For civic chauvinism's sake, even Milwaukee is windier than we are, with an 11.5 mph average. Still, every time the wind whips up—it's windiest in January, March, and April; least so in July, August, and September—you'll hear tourists and locals alike tossing around the Windy City name.

It is not as if the city doesn't have other colorful nicknames. We are the Second City (the result of A. J. Liebling's stories in the *New Yorker* in the 1950s). We are the City of the Big Shoulders and Hog Butcher for the World (courtesy of Carl Sandburg). We are the City That Works (loose credit to Mayor Richard J. Daley) and the City on the Make (courtesy of Nelson Algren).

But of them all, Windy City is the most frequently employed—the most popular. Part of the reason lies with some of us in the newspaper business. In the last couple of years, writers have used the term hundreds of times in the pages of the *Tribune,* offering such sentences as "Winter officially arrived Monday with a bluster and a chill that did little to dampen the spirits of procrastinating holiday shoppers and visitors to the Windy City" and "Far from maddening Madison Avenue, the world's largest ad agency, which happens to be headquartered in the Land of the Rising Sun, has discovered the Windy City." Headline writers are not immune to Windy City-itis, giving us: "Fog City Diner Finds Its Way to Windy City"; "Stones Can't Resist Another Date with the Windy City"; and "Another TV Series Has Windy City Written All Over It."

There is another reason the phrase remains so deeply embedded. It is that so many businesses have eagerly adopted it. There are dozens of them, from Windy City Air to Windy City 2 Steppers. Some of my favorites are Windy City Cat Sitters, Windy City Gyros II, Windy City Ink and Iron, Windy City Foam, and Windy City Comics Inc. There is a newspaper, *Windy City Times,* and a magazine, *Windy City Sports.* There are five Windy City Video operations. A Windy City Wrestling Hotline. There is a Windy City Car Wash, which should not be confused with Windy City Car Wash and Detail. There is, thank God, a Windy City Woodstripper and Gut Out Service.

And so we stood, Osgood and I, waiting for the sort of decent gust of wind that might give us the right look for a story about wind. (The highest recorded wind speed in Chicago is 58 mph in September 1952. The highest gust was 69 mph in 1984.) While we waited, I struggled to recall this area's first nickname. Finally, I remembered: Checagou, an Indian word meant to signify anything big, strong, or powerful, in that case used to describe the odor of the skunk cabbage and wild onion that grew on the banks of what is now called the Chicago River.

Checagou Woodstripper and Gut Out Service. Has a nice ring, don't you think?

MAY 2, 1999

A NOVEL GARDEN

THE GHOSTS OF THE CITY'S PAST have a way of being thrust into the present, with names of dead people affixed to parks, streets, harbors. Most of the names are familiar. Some are less so, such as the one attached to a rectangular space at Haddon Avenue and Wood Street. That name is Frank Majcinek, but he is better known as Frankie Machine, the title character of *The Man with the Golden Arm,* the 1949 novel by Chicago's Nelson Algren.

In the last days of winter, the garden had a haggard look that is typical this time of year. Of the dozen or so people who strolled past on a day so sunny and springlike that it might have commanded flowers to instantly start blooming, none could identify Frankie Machine. No one knew that he was a tragic figure, a poker-dealing dope addict. In the novel, Machine's apartment was near where the garden now sits, and many of the poker games he dealt took place in smoky rooms on Division Street, one block north.

The garden is one of about sixty such oases that dot the city. It was started in 1988 by members of the East Village Association; its name resulted from a name-the-garden contest. The space was originally divided into fourteen plots and began to come ablaze yearly with flowers, herbs, fruits, and vegetables. The land was purchased in 1998 by NeighborSpace, a nonprofit trust formed in 1996 and principally funded by the Chicago Park District, the City of Chicago, and the Forest Preserve District of Cook County.

"The group in charge of this garden is incredibly well organized," says NeighborSpace's executive director, Marcia Davis. There are now twenty-one plots in the garden and a waiting list for spaces. "Being involved with the garden is something I consider one of the greatest accomplishments in my life," says Marjorie Isaacson, the garden's manager.

What would Algren make of this small park, this garden in the city?

"He's not what I'd think of as the gardening type," says Isaacson, a data manager and research project organizer at the University of Chicago. "But it does honor him."

I like to think that Algren, who was a close friend of my parents and who has a portion of nearby Evergreen Avenue named in his honor, would get a kick out of the garden. He'd be a lot happier about it than about the recent renaming of a block of Bellevue Place in honor of Frank Sinatra. In the film version of *The Man with the Golden Arm,* Sinatra played Machine. Algren hated that movie.

APRIL 6, 2000

WHEN IN ROMA'S

IT IS PROBABLY IMPOSSIBLE to accurately calculate the number of Italian beef or hot dog joints in the city. They come and go as rapidly as summer afternoon thunderstorms.

I was introduced to Roma's in the early 1970s, thanks to the dining tastes of high school pal Al Placek, whose family lived nearby on Lamon Avenue. I was hooked, though it was never close to the neighborhoods in which I've lived. It was owned by Ron Sommario and his parents, who bought it in 1973 after the hot dog stand they'd run since 1948 at Loomis and Cabrini Streets fell to make way for the University of Illinois at Chicago.

I've been to Roma's dozens of times and at all hours over the decades, and Ron has always been there behind the counter at 4237 North Cicero Avenue. He's ever amiable and always points out a framed news clipping on the wall, a small story I wrote about the place back in 1974, containing the gentle prices of those days: Italian beef sandwich, with peppers and tax, was ninety-five cents; a hot dog was sixty cents.

Things change. Sommario's hair has gone from dark to gray. Prices have gone up. Help is not as easy to find or as reliable as it once was.

On my most recent trip to Roma's—where we met Lucy (from left), Rolando, Nick, and Alex Lopez—I noticed a new sign for the Bob Collins Special: a beef-sausage combo with fries and a large Diet Pepsi.

"I miss him terribly," said Sommario, who first met the late WGN radio star more than twenty years ago. "He'd come here every week, sometimes more than once, and we became great pals. We'd go out to dinner, go on trips together. And he was a great friend of my family."

Sommario and his wife have raised five children, but it is unlikely that any of them will take over the business when Ron retires. "They all worked here as kids, and now four of them are out of school and working in other businesses. None of them want any part of this," he says. "They've seen how hard the job is. They want to take vacations."

Sommario hasn't taken more than a couple of days off for more than four years, but he still seems to love what he does. He's always friendly, though reluctant to give away the recipes that make his fare distinctively tasty.

In that story I wrote many years ago, I told of a man who ate, in one sitting, fourteen beef sandwiches. At the time, Sommario made an offer: eat fourteen beef sandwiches and the fifteenth is free.

That's one thing that hasn't changed. "Oh, you bet. That offer still stands," Ron said.

AUGUST 20, 2000

STILL TOUGH

WHEN I FIRST MET Fred Degerberg, he was walking down Wells Street in the company of John Belushi late one night in the summer of 1980, two years before the actor's death. Degerberg was an intimidating-looking fellow, with a shaved head, menacing mustache, and steely eyes. He sometimes provided security for Belushi and other stars in town, but he was also Belushi's martial arts instructor.

"John was a Bruce Lee fanatic," says Degerberg. "He was also a very good athlete and a good student."

Belushi trained at the school Degerberg still operates, the Degerberg Academy, at 4717 North Lincoln Avenue, where Osgood took the accompanying photo (that's Fred, with the white beard). It is a vast complex, the number one martial arts school in the country, according to the United States Martial Arts Association. Tens of thousands of students have trained there in such familiar martial arts as karate, kung fu, judo, jujitsu, aikido, wrestling, and boxing as well as exotic pursuits like arnis, kali, bando, and jeet kune do. "Over the years we've taught two hundred different styles of martial arts," says Degerberg. "That's why I like to refer to it as a martial arts university."

When Degerberg, the son of a wrestler and the grandson of a boxer, took up martial arts some fifty years ago, it was, he says, "kind of a weird thing to do, but I've watched it become mainstream. When I started, there were virtually no women in the martial arts. Now they represent more than fifty percent in some of the classes."

Last year, Degerberg took over a school that had been in business for thirty-eight years at 3596 North Milwaukee Avenue. It's a beautiful space with a Japanese garden out back with a waterfall, pond, and trees.

"I still love to teach, especially beginners," he says. "The martial arts still turn me on."

Recalling what he looked like twenty-five years ago, we had to ask, "Are you still tough?"

"I'm a little softer in the middle than I was," he said. "But for thirty seconds, I'd be your worst nightmare."

NOVEMBER 6, 2005

WORDS TO LIVE BY

THE ROAD FROM GLENBROOK NORTH HIGH SCHOOL in the early 1990s to an El stop in the Near Southwest Side neighborhood of Pilsen may not fit conventional notions of a career path, but it's been a rewarding journey so far for Kevin Coval.

Two days short of his twenty-ninth birthday, he is one of the area's most intriguing "hyphenates": poet-emcee-activist-performer-essayist-educator. Judging his writing talent is, of course, a subjective exercise, but no one can argue with his success and growing influence. He is one of the featured poets in *The Spoken Word Revolution: Slam, Hip Hop, and the Poetry of a New Generation,* edited by Mark Eleveld and Marc Smith; cofounded the Chicago Teen Poetry Slam; works with Young Chicago Authors, which teaches creative writing to young people; teaches at the Francis W. Parker School in the Lincoln Park neighborhood and conducts workshops at many other high schools and colleges; has read his ode to the city, "Love Letter to Chicago," on WBEZ radio; and has appeared on *Def Poetry Jam* on HBO. He also oversees Louder Than a Bomb, the annual Chicago Teen Poetry Festival in which more than thirty teams compete.

Not bad for a Jewish kid from Northbrook whose parents ran a restaurant and who began listening to hip-hop before he was ten. Later, greatly influenced by such books as *The Autobiography of Malcolm X,* he turned his back on his religion, but over the years he has used hip-hop to explore and come to terms with his background. (He has published a collection of poems entitled *Pieces of Shalom.*) He now has a New York agent who has helped get him gigs in such places as South Africa, India, and Europe—and who must have cringed when his client turned down twenty thousand dollars to appear in a beer commercial as a "Chicago poet."

One day Coval hopes to return to college; he spent a couple of years working on a degree in religious studies at DePaul University. But it's hard to imagine when he'd find time.

He believes that all kids, no matter where they are from, have stories to tell and that "the power of the spoken word enables us to see beyond the traditional distinctions of race." In this increasingly screwed-up world, those sound like important, maybe even essential, words to live by.

MARCH 21, 2004

MEET THE DOUGHNUT MAN

ROSELAND, THE SOUTH SIDE NEIGHBORHOOD, is where in November 1972 Buritt Bulloch and his wife, Mamie, decided to open a business.

"I had heard that Roseland was a good place for family-run businesses," Bulloch says. "When I was looking at the building I moved into [at 11248 South Michigan Avenue], a man told me that every business that had been there had been a success."

Bulloch's business was and is making doughnuts, and there are those who will tell you that Old Fashioned Doughnuts makes the best. Naturally, Bulloch likes to hear such praise.

"I have a lot of loyal customers," he says. "A lot of people who moved out of the neighborhood still come back here for their doughnuts."

From the beginning Bulloch also operated a grill, serving hot dogs, hamburgers, and other food. He also has shakes and ice cream. "Some people, they don't have as big a taste for doughnuts when it's ninety-five degrees," he says.

A native of northern Mississippi, Bulloch learned to make doughnuts during the many years he worked here for the Amy Joy company. He saved his money. He opened his shop.

Unlike many of the small business owners that Osgood and I meet, Bulloch is not resentful of the larger chains that cut into their territory.

"Oh, that Dunkin' Donuts was around here long before I opened," he says, with quiet confidence. "They make a pretty good doughnut. And even that Krispy Kreme that's new around here, they started a long time ago in the South."

Krispy Kreme has all but destroyed Bulloch's once-thriving business with local schools, which used to buy dozens of his doughnuts for fund-raisers.

"But that's okay," he says. "They don't make a bad doughnut, but some people think they are sort of on the small side."

Bulloch's doughnuts are comparatively huge and as good as you will find anywhere. That's the reason he sells about two hundred dozen a day. His secret?

"Just hard work, I guess," he says.

NOVEMBER 2, 2003

THERE REALLY IS a Lake Claremont. It is in Western Australia, about as far from Chicago as one can get. But Lake Claremont Press has nothing to do with Australia and everything to do with Chicago. In its offices on North Rockwell Street, you can clearly hear the El's roar and clatter.

Over the last ten years, this small publishing house has turned out nearly thirty titles, all of them focusing on the city, including *Great Chicago Fires, Chicago's Midway Airport, Literary Chicago, A Cook's Guide to Chicago,* and *The Chicago River.* This year the firm is publishing six books (actually five books and one audiobook). Among them is a new edition of *A Native's Guide to Chicago,* the book that started it all.

Sharon Woodhouse, the young lady in the photo, wrote that book and decided to publish it herself in 1994. "I was kind of thrown into this whole thing," she says. "I was in graduate school at UIC studying philosophy, and I never expected to become a successful publisher."

LOCAL LITERATURE

The company's philosophy is this: "Preserving the past. Exploring the present. Ensuring a future sense of place for our corner of the world." In addition to Woodhouse, there are one full-time and two part-time employees, and each year they field about 250 pitches from authors, everything from finished manuscripts to "I've got an idea for a book and what should I do?" phone calls.

Arnie Bernstein has had three fine books published by Lake Claremont. The most recent is *The Hoofs and Guns of the Storm: Chicago's Civil War Connections.*

"Sharon genuinely loves this city," he says. "She's given me great opportunities to explore my own passions for Chicago history. There aren't enough good words in the dictionary to praise what she's accomplished."

If you ever happen to meet Woodhouse, ask her about the origin of her company's name. It is, as if you couldn't guess, another good Chicago story.

JUNE 6, 2002

SALOONS IN THE SKY

THE WORLD CAN LOOK DIFFERENT when you are drunk. It can look better than it is or it can look worse, depending on your mood, the amount of booze you've had to drink, and the place in which you've been drinking it. Most saloons do what they can to fight off dark thoughts by offering all sorts of what might be considered lively distractions: a jukebox or live band; dart boards, pool tables, or video games; or attractive members of the opposite sex.

But the world changes immediately when you're sitting on a stool in the Signature Lounge, on the ninety-sixth floor of the hundred-story John Hancock Center. The world is different even before you take your first sip. The city, from the sky, is an unreal place. Below, things move, but life appears cheap. Below, people are toiling and loving, crying and dying. From the sky, the city's personal landmarks fade into the anonymous patchwork. Visibility on this day is relatively poor, only ten miles, through a soupy haze. The lake lies flat, unruffled. On top of a Streeterville high-rise, a man—it looks like a man—swims alone in the bright blue water of a swimming pool.

"It's better at night," one man tells the woman whose hand he is holding. "All the lights."

"Then why are we here now?" she asks.

The Hancock Center was completed in 1970. It is arguably the city's most recognizable structure. Look closely, outside the windows. See the spiders spinning webs on the skin of the building? How did they get up here? Carried by the wind, obviously, since the climb would certainly have taken them a lifetime.

There are many people who find the Hancock's bar romantic; the sunsets have prompted many proposals of marriage and other liaisons. Others come here because they would rather invest the money it costs to get into the Hancock Observatory (two floors below) in a cocktail. This is not a place frequented by many locals. The people in Osgood's photo are from Norway. What self-respecting Chicagoan would order the Skyscraper, made with lemon-flavored rum and pineapple and cranberry juices? But it is a good place, if not as famous as some other sky saloons. The Top of the Mark in the InterContinental Mark Hopkins Hotel in San Francisco is very stylish and has great views, but, c'mon, it's only on the nineteenth floor.

And there was once a place called Windows on the World. More restaurant than bar, it served a great martini and offered stunning views from atop one of the towers of the World Trade Center. It is impossible not to recall drinking in the sky in New York while drinking in the sky in Chicago, feeling better about the world because we're still in it—and yet worse.

NOVEMBER 14, 2004

WRITTEN ON THE ROCKS

ON THE LAKEFRONT near Belmont Avenue, people have written poems on the rocks. No one really knows how long this has been going on, and in the many times Osgood and I have visited this stretch of craggy shoreline, we have not seen anyone writing poems on the rocks or met anyone who has seen anyone else writing poems on the rocks.

Some of the poems are original and some are those of famous poets; some are not poems at all but words from the Bible or private messages. But all of this rock writing, it seems to me, represents a collective and gentle cry in the urban wilderness, a sort of grown-up version of putting your handprint in wet cement or scratching your initials and those of a lover (or crush) inside a heart on the bark of a tree. They represent the various ways in which some people say, in a world increasingly e-mail icy, "I was here!"

The last time I went to look at the writing on the rocks I was toting a collection of poetry titled *The Art of Drowning,* published in 1995 and written by Billy Collins. I had picked up the book earlier in the day because I was curious to read something by Collins, who had recently been named the U.S. poet laureate, a thirty-five-thousand-dollar-a-year job he began with a reading at the Library of Congress in Washington, D.C. I picked up his collection because I liked the way Collins reacted when told of his appointment, saying it "came completely out of the blue, like a soft wrecking ball from outer space." I also like the ordinariness of his name, Billy Collins, as if he were a ballplayer or something.

So there I was, reading the collection and being especially taken with the title poem, which begins, "I wonder how it all got started, this business / about seeing your life flash before your eyes / while you drown." In pondering this, he later suggests, "But if something does flash before your eyes / as you go under, it will probably be a fish, / a quick blur of curved silver darting away, / having nothing to do with your life or your death."

I had earlier passed a couple of guys fishing near Diversey Harbor; also joggers, skaters, strollers, dogs, lovers, sailors. Perhaps one was a secret rock writer. All of them had everything to do with life.

AUGUST 19, 2001

EATING AT JOE'S

THE EXCLUSIVE KITCHEN MUSEUM of Evanston is wedged into a corner of an Evanston restaurant at 1921 Central Street and consists solely of kitchen clocks from the 1950s and 1960s. This is in keeping with the wild decorative theme of Prairie Joe's, which is a time capsule of sorts—with rotary phones, portable record players, vintage salt and pepper shakers, movie projectors, old cameras, record albums, Formica tables with vinyl chairs, and all manner of artwork, including a plastic shark hanging from the ceiling. The eye can hardly catch it all.

The owner and chef of Prairie Joe's is Aydin Dincer, himself an artist who has spent more than twenty years in the kitchens of such high-end joints as Jilly's (just around the corner on Green Bay Road) and Printers Row in Chicago's South Loop. In 1985 he opened Star Top, a Lincoln Avenue restaurant that, even with its risky menu, was a deliciously homespun place and, in memory, a continuing glimmer. Prairie Joe's was Jordan's when Dincer took over in 1991. He redecorated and gave the menu a sophisticated spin. But he did not alarm or otherwise put off longtime customers.

Bill Rusch has been a regular for thirty years. Every morning he meets eight or nine pals from the neighborhood for breakfast. On the walls you can see their faces in framed photos or, in Rusch's case, a painted portrait. It is the work of another regular, a self-taught artist named Ed Wuytack, whose carvings of birds and airplanes are also on view. Of his portrait Rusch says, with terse modesty, "I don't mind it."

This sort of spot—the word "diner" comes most quickly to mind—is becoming harder to find in this homogenized and hurried world. Another cup of coffee? Oh, no. I've got a meeting. A place of quiet surprises—for the eyes and the palate—it is also a comfortable study in playful informality.

JANUARY 24, 1999

HOOKED ON ICE

IT IS ONE OF SUMMER'S special rites, practiced by all manner of people, such as a smiling forty-year-old named Jeff Gibbs, who one day in June was standing in line in front of Mario's Italian Lemonade, at 1068 West Taylor Street. It may not seem like much, this little one-story wooden shack, painted a happy red and white. But for many, a trip to Mario's Italian Lemonade is as important as a visit to a religious shrine.

"It's the best ice around," Gibbs was saying.

A crowd of students arrived in front of the shack. They milled about, talking about picking a flavor to eat. This can get complicated. There are sixteen flavors of ice at Mario's.

"Cherry," said a female student.

"Lemon," said a male student. "I am what you might call a traditionalist."

"That's just another word for boring," said a female student, and the kids all laughed.

Generations ago in this neighborhood and a couple of others, there were ice stands or carts on almost every corner. There are fewer now, though each has its loyalists. Mario's does a frantic business from May to September. On warm days the line down the sidewalk is so long it might convince a person that Mario's was giving something away. The customers are a wonderful mix, and they mix wonderfully, if only for as long as it takes to share a line and order an ice. It is as if they are all, for a moment, members of the same club.

"Happy summer," said a firefighter as he walked across the street, raising his cup as if it were a cocktail and he were making a toast.

"You too," said Andre Cooper, the man in the picture. He is a minister at a West Side Baptist church, and he comes to Mario's with his family once or twice a week.

"You've got to have ices in the summer," he said. "They're especially good when they melt down."

The most popular flavors are lemon, watermelon, and cantaloupe. This information was provided by eighteen-year-old Nariana Ramirez, one of a number of teenage girls who pleasantly and efficiently serve customers.

"What, no boys work here?" I asked.

"We don't allow them," she said, smiling. "No, they're in the back, cutting the fruit . . . Next in line, please. What flavor? What size?"

JULY 11, 1999

ONE RECENT AFTERNOON, ten born-and-raised Chicagoans could not identify the person for whom the street they were about to cross was named. A few of them, even as they were looking up at the street sign, said, in what has become a common Chicago mispronunciation, "Balboa."

It is Balbo, named for an Italian air minister, General Italo Balbo, who in 1933 led a flock of twenty-four seaplanes here for the Century of Progress Exposition. Antifascist groups protested the idea of naming a street in his honor, but their cries did not stop Seventh Street from becoming Balbo Drive. It begins (or ends, depending on your point of view) at Grant Park, named at the turn of the century for the Civil War general and U.S. president, Ulysses S.

In this area of Grant Park along Michigan Avenue stands an impressive statue of John Alexander Logan, a Civil War general who later represented Illinois in Congress. (His name also labels a boulevard, a plaza, and an entire neighborhood.) It is impossible for many Chicagoans to look at the statue of Logan and the greenery that surrounds it

THE BATTLE OF BALBO

and not be swept back to August 1968 and the events that took place then and there.

That was the month the Democrats came to town; for the first time since 1956, Chicago had been chosen as the site of the Democratic National Convention. Mayor Richard J. Daley said this was "an important sign of faith to the American people for this national convention to be held here, not in some resort center, but in the very heart of a great city, where people live and work and raise their families."

His enthusiasm and pride, however, were shadowed by worry. He was not concerned, as one might think given the way things turned out, about the war protesters and other long-haired "agitators" expected to come to town. Daley knew their principal weapons were only words. One forgets that the people he most feared might upset the convention were blacks, his paranoia fueled by the riots earlier in the year that devastated portions of the West Side in the wake of the April assassination of Martin Luther King Jr. So it was decided that police would pressure various black militants and gang members, arresting some and hassling others—getting across the behave-or-else message.

But Daley's political savvy dictated a less aggressive maneuver, and on August 1, 1968, the city council met to placate the black community by renaming a street in honor of King. Many descriptions of this meeting have been written. None better captured it than Mike Royko in his biography of Daley called *Boss:* "The meeting was remarkable, with one administration alderman after another eulogizing King as a great man, forgetting that they had assailed him when he was

alive. Daley himself described his relationship with King as one of great friendship and mutual understanding, claiming that King had told him what a fine job he was doing for the city's blacks. The heights to which Daley and the aldermen rose in praising King moved one observer to write: 'It was enough to bring tears to your eyes, if you happened to be a crocodile.' "

The street selected for the name change was South Park Way, which ran through predominantly black sections of the South Side. There were suggestions, Royko wrote, that the street chosen cut through the whole city (Western Avenue, perhaps), but Daley wouldn't listen. He knew that in white neighborhoods street signs would be defaced or destroyed. So South Park Way became Dr. Martin Luther King Jr. Drive, and a few weeks later the Democrats came to town. And what most remember is what happened on August 28—it was a Wednesday—when protesters and police clashed in Grant Park.

The skirmishes between these groups on previous convention nights in Lincoln Park may have been as bloody, but they did not have the dubious distinction of television cameras present to record the action: the world was watching. It lasted only about twenty minutes; 101 demonstrators were hospitalized, and 192 police officers reported injuries. A national commission headed by future Illinois governor Dan Walker later deemed the melee a "police riot," but Daley was unscathed. This was because, as Royko put it in *Boss*, "In attacking the young, the liberal, and the black, Daley was in the mainstream of America's mass prejudices . . . Daley came out of the convention even more popular than before because 'bust their heads' was the mood of the land and Daley had swung the biggest club."

For a time the August 28 confrontation was called the Battle of Balbo, but soon it was most commonly referred to as the Battle of Chicago—Balbo, of course, being too obscure a name for permanence.

These days, Grant Park is a peaceful place, its most disruptive moments taking place when ravenous mobs descend on it during Taste of Chicago. These days, people lounge at the base of General Logan's statue. Little kids try to climb the horse's legs as they would metal trees. In 1968 protesters tried to climb the Logan statue and were peeled from it by police. In the heat of the night, ironies and history escaped the demonstrators. There they were, trying to stop a war in Vietnam while trying to scale the statue of a man who, a hundred years before, had come up with an idea for remembering men who died in war.

His idea was Memorial Day. But perhaps you already knew that.

AUGUST 30, 1998

WHAT'S FOR *FROKOST*?

I DO NOT OFTEN GET a taste for Scandinavian food, primarily because, beyond the familiar Swedish pancakes and Swedish meatballs, I don't know much about the cuisines of Norway, Denmark, or Sweden. But leave it to Osgood, who could find a sandwich shop in the Sahara, to discover as fine a Scandinavian restaurant as there is in the city, a charming place called Tre Kronor, at 3258 West Foster Avenue.

It is a small storefront outpost, crisp and clean, with twenty or so tables, walls filled with pictures of Scandinavia, and a mural with strange-looking children and trolls. It was painted in 1986 by the late local Norwegian American artist Reidar Rosenvinge.

"The mural doesn't tell a story or a fable, it's just cute characters," says Larry Anderson, a Swedish American from Berwyn. He has owned and operated the restaurant with his wife, Patricia Rasmussen, whose ancestry is Norwegian, since 1992. The couple—that's Patricia with baby Maggie in Osgood's photo—has created a menu that is an interesting blend of Scandinavian tastes and those more provincial.

Osgood and I were there for breakfast—*frokost* in Swedish—and had a hard time selecting from the menu. I tried to make Osgood have a Stockholm omelette (*falukov* sausage and caraway Havarti cheese) or an Oslo omelette (smoked salmon, dill, and cream cheese). He opted for the French toast while I ate hash and eggs. Both quite tasty.

The place was bright and sunny, with a pleasant view of part of the North Park University campus across Foster Avenue. The university, if you didn't know, was founded by first-generation Swedish Americans in the 1890s, which helps explain the Swedish feel of the area: Swedish Covenant Hospital a few blocks to the east and the Swedish Shop, a large gift store, a few feet to the west.

Tre Kronor, which means "three crowns" in Swedish, is also open for lunch and dinner. Osgood wanted to stay there until lunch, eager to try the Norwegian meatball sandwich, but I persuaded him to go back to the office, promising that we would return someday for blueberry soup, which is best served and slurped chilled on hot summer days.

APRIL 30, 2000

DUBIOUS HONORS

INEVITABLY, THERE WILL BE a Charles Osgood Way. The city is filled with street signs that honor accomplished Chicagoans and all sorts of others, so why not Osgood? Or me? Or you? How about Mrs. Kim, who owns my neighborhood dry cleaner?

If you think this all a bit silly, look at the sign in Osgood's picture. It is right in front of the Tribune Tower on Michigan Avenue.

"Ridiculous," said Osgood.

"Insane," said I.

A couple of years ago, *Tribune* columnist Eric Zorn called for the removal of all honorary street signs, calling them "goofy, small town and way out of hand." At the time, the city was slapping up about 80 or so a year. The city council responded to Zorn's courageous and correct call by approving a record 103 honorary street designations in 2000 and the following year broke that record with another 120.

Most of the time there's no one to complain. And who wants to argue against making the street sign gesture to the late Jack Brickhouse?

The biggest flap took place in the spring of 2000 when a sign went up on the northwest corner of Walton Street and Michigan Avenue. Hugh M. Hefner Way outraged many who didn't think the creator of *Playboy* deserved the "honor." But up the sign went. Nothing against Hefner or any of the others whose names are affixed to light poles, but what's the point, really? Does anyone ever use the honorary names? Have you ever been asked, for instance, to meet someone at the corner of Paul Harvey and Michigan?

I used to live on a street named for a tree, and many of you live on streets named for U.S. presidents. But other street names have fascinating, almost hidden histories. Rollicking Rush Street, for instance, was named for Benjamin Rush, one of four doctors to sign the Declaration of Independence.

A wonderful book published more than a decade ago cataloged the origins of the names of the city's 1,101 byways. The only street name that *Streetwise Chicago* authors Don Hayner and Tom McNamee couldn't pin down was Agatite Avenue. Perhaps that could be renamed in honor of the Bears' Brian Urlacher. It's about time, isn't it?

SEPTEMBER 1, 2002

THE QUICK BROWN FOX

IF YOU HAVE NEVER HEARD IT or if it has been pushed from your brain by the soulless tapping of computer keys, the sound of typewriter keys banging is a beautiful noise. There is not a newspaper person of a certain age who does not feel this way. A typewriter's sound is able to evoke the charming chaos that used to exist in newsrooms. It is the sound of effort, of work.

I heard this sound again in the small Montrose Avenue storefront shop of a man named Steve Kazmier. The windows were filled with about thirty machines, and dozens more were on the shelves inside, looking new and ready to feel the touch of fingers. Kazmier was in his workroom in the back of the tiny shop.

"Computers are my enemy," he said.

On many days the only living creatures to walk through the door of the store are two pigeons that Kazmier has befriended and feeds from a bag of corn he keeps near his desk. He is, he will tell you, "a dinosaur, one of the last of my breed." He came to the United States from Germany in 1950, and his first job was in the repair department of the bygone International Typewriter Exchange. He has been working with typewriters ever since, even during the two years he spent in the air force. In 1964 he began working out of the south suburban home he shared with his wife and three children. As computers began to replace typewriters, Kazmier decided he needed to be more visible and opened his shop in 1990. It has been a tough decade.

"At first I was getting fifteen, sixteen calls a day to do work," he said. "Now, maybe two calls a month."

Still, he is determined to hang on.

"There is a need for typewriters because there are a lot of forms that need to be typed so that they can be read by computers," he said. "And I am selling some typewriters to young writers. They like the feel of the keys, the sound of the keys."

He sells some typewriters, older models mainly, to people who use them as art objects.

"The best typewriter ever made was the IBM Selectric," he said. "But these older models have a romance to them. This, this is the same style typewriter Hemingway used to write on."

He slipped a piece of paper into the black Royal and began to play its keys. It was music. Or maybe it was magic for this man of rare talents.

OCTOBER 3, 1999

212

A TOUCH OF THE PAST

IVANHOE SITS IN unincorporated Lake County near the intersection of Illinois Highways 83 and 176. It is, like so many suburban areas, undergoing rapid changes as "progress" transforms farms into shopping malls, hills into parking lots, and, in the process, history into dust.

But bulldozers and developers do not as easily mess with eternity, so you will find there a lovely place known as Ivanhoe Cemetery. It was born—I know that's an odd choice of word, but it is still appropriate—more than a century and a half ago when settlers moved into the area, and it continues in operation to this day.

"We just added another acre to the north," says Dorothy Dolph, who acts as the cemetery's secretary-treasurer, one of a number of volunteers who keep the grounds spruced up and in operation. Originally from Chicago, Dolph now lives in nearby Mundelein, adding that "I have only lived here since 1951 when I got married." Her husband's name is Myron and, Dorothy says with considerable pride, "five generations of his family are buried in the Ivanhoe Cemetery."

Osgood and I have always been fond of cemeteries. They don't scare us but rather provide shelter from the urban hustle and seem to us fascinating sculpture gardens shadowed by history. The Ivanhoe Cemetery, for instance, was once affiliated with the nearby Ivanhoe Congregational Church, and it was in 1850 that members of the congregation's sewing circle raised the money to build the first fence for the graveyard.

The grave in Osgood's photo has a story. When one of the area's residents returned from fighting in the Civil War, he was in the company of a free slave named James Joice, who later sent for his wife and family. Here they lived, one of the first black clans to do so.

As "progress" remakes the surrounding landscape, Ivanhoe Cemetery remains a place where one can not only remember but touch the past.

MARCH 2, 2003

IT MUST MEAN SOMETHING when Osgood and Tim Weigel, the sportscaster, are both in love with the same woman. That woman is Bonnie Koloc, and Chicago is littered with men and women who are in love with her—or at least with the sound of her voice as they might remember it from long ago when she was a frequent presence on Chicago stages.

Koloc does not often perform in Chicago these days. She and her husband, writer Robert Wolf, who recently published an amazing book called *An American Mosaic: Prose and Poetry by Everyday Folk,* live in the northeastern corner of Iowa.

It is always jarring to see Wolf in an urban setting because, though he did a lot of writing for the *Tribune* some time back, he has been living a rural life for years with Bonnie. For more than a decade Wolf has been getting people to tell him stories, and the harvest is rich and satisfying. The people in *An American Mosaic* are homeless and day laborers, farmers and teachers,

LOVING BONNIE

college students and commercial fishermen. They met Wolf during the many writing workshops he conducts. He gets people to attend by telling them that "anyone who can tell a story can write one."

That's a bold theory, but the book is filled with wonderful stories. Almost all are interesting, and some are poetic. Here's a bit from a story by a farmer named Richard Sandry: "We finally get home and just as we come into the house, the rain begins to fall. Shortly, the full fury of the storm is upon us. As I watch, looking out through the window, I think of how the days of my life go. How the clouds on the horizon of my sunrises sometimes, later in the day, turn into the black clouds of fear, of despair, of anger, of uncertainty, and of depression."

The stories in the book, and essays and commentary by Wolf, are funny, sad, and meaningful. They offer insights into the lives of people and of places that many of us, caught up in the frenetic pace of city life, forget exist. They are of small towns and quiet lives.

The book also contains lovely artwork by Bonnie. I know what you are thinking: Why do people think they can do something other than what they do best? Michael Jordan playing baseball?! But that is not the case with Bonnie. Art was her major in college, and her work—ink drawings, block prints, and photographic collages—is stunning. But remembering the first times I saw Koloc and one night when Weigel and I were brought to tears by her singing, I walked over to Wells Street and stared wistfully into the saloon that used to be the Earl of Old Town. I thought of Steve Goodman and John Prine and realized all over again that I loved Bonnie, too.

MARCH 26, 2000

OF BULLETS AND BRICKS

A FENCE EXTENDS along a portion of the west side of the 2100 block of North Clark Street, surrounding a piece of ground at the edge of a retirement home. It is the sort of city space that few ever notice, but this is the site of the St. Valentine's Day Massacre, as the 1929 slaughter of seven men by the gun-toting minions of Al Capone has become fancifully known.

For decades after the crime, on any given day, one could find groups of kids staring at the two-story building with its Werner Storage sign, imagining past mayhem inside, picturing what happened that bygone morning at about 10:30 A.M., when four men burst into the SMC Cartage Company garage at 2122 North Clark Street. The place was being used by Capone rival George "Bugs" Moran for various illegal doings, most notably those of his bootlegging enterprise.

Two of the men who entered the building were dressed as police officers, and they ordered the seven men inside the garage—six Moran associates and Reinhardt Schwimmer, an optometrist who got his kicks hanging out with mobsters—to line up against a whitewashed brick wall. Immediately the intruders opened fire, spraying the wall and the seven men with more than one hundred bullets. For six of the victims, the time of death was noted on police reports as 10:40 A.M. Frank Gusenberg, a top Moran aide, lived for nearly three more hours, even though there were fourteen bullets in his body. Dying but blindly adhering to that code of honor among hoodlums, Gusenberg refused to tell his pal, Sergeant Thomas J. Loftus of the old Thirty-sixth District, who had done the shooting. But everyone knew. "Only Capone kills like that," said Moran. No one was ever tried for the crime, but it worked its way firmly into the city's history and its image.

When the old garage was demolished in 1967, a Canadian named George Patey purchased a seven-and-a-half-foot-wide-by-eleven-foot-high section of the bullet-riddled north wall. The price has never been disclosed, but the bricks, 417 of them, were numbered, packed in barrels, and shipped to Patey. (Seven bricks were missing.)

The wall became a traveling exhibit, but the public decried it. A museum wouldn't take it off Patey's hands, and eventually it was installed in the men's room of the Banjo Palace, a Roaring Twenties–style saloon Patey owned. In 1996 Patey and his associate, E. W. "Bill" Eliason, tried to auction off the wall for two hundred thousand dollars. They got a few offers, but none serious. Last year they hooked up with an Internet site that offered individual bricks for one thousand dollars. In five days, sixty-eight were ordered, but the company went bust before any bricks were delivered.

FEBRUARY 14, 1999

A WINNING MEAL TICKET

EVERY YEAR FOR MORE THAN TWENTY YEARS I have made it a point around the holidays to visit Bridgeport. Perhaps it is because I remember the bitterly cold December day in 1976 when Eleanor "Sis" Daley stood and shook hands with virtually everyone who came to pay their respects to her late husband, Richard J.

Or perhaps it's just because I find Bridgeport such an interesting place, historically and currently. Poet and writer John Aranza, who lives on Thirty-second Street and is passionate about his neighborhood, once wrote of Morgan Street that it "conveyed the feeling of a little village to itself, an 'Our Town,' a world of its own."

Or, as Mike Royko wrote in his definitive portrait of the neighborhood's favorite son, *Boss*: "In Bridgeport's early days, the people grew cabbage on vacant land in their yards, and it was known for a time as the Cabbage Patch. But by the time Daley was born, most people had stopped raising cabbage and had taken to raising politicians. Daley was to become the third consecutive mayor produced by Bridgeport. It would also produce an extraordinary number of lesser office-holders, appointed officials, and, legend says, even more votes than it had voters."

I have no idea what strange faces some of the area's previous residents might have made upon finding baked Brie en croûte on the menu at Polo Café and Catering, at 3322 South Morgan Street, but this is one of the city's hidden treasures. Carved from what was once the city's oldest confectionery, the restaurant is as friendly as any in town and has extraordinary food from a simple fish-pasta-beef menu given inventive twists by owner and chef Dave Samber.

It's a small place with booths, tables, and a colorful mural of the neighborhood and portraits of those local guys who were mayor before Richard J. Daley, Edward Kelly and Martin Kennelly, and a couple who came after him, Michael Bilandic and Richard M. Daley.

Samber is a former North Sider who moved here and opened the place in 1985. His catering business is small but steady, and there is a healthy holiday business with gift baskets and trays of homemade cookies and other goodies.

Samber will happily tell you the history of the place and the neighborhood and will take you next door into the striking space he has created from what was once a Lithuanian movie house. The Old Eagle Room features a lovely organ, a stage, and the item Samber is holding in Osgood's photo: a gizmo that allows lights to dance across the walls, floor, and ceiling.

It may be some time before Bridgeport produces another mayor, but in the Polo Café it has an ongoing winner.

JANUARY 13, 2002

THE WAY THINGS WERE

IT HAPPENED WHEN AN AUTO REPAIR SHOP was leveled to make way for a new condominium development. There, on one side of the building at 1914 West Irving Park Road, was a fading advertisement revealed for the first time in decades.

"It's terrible," said a neighborhood resident. "Just a horrible thing."

The ad featured, as you can see, two half-dressed caricatures doing housework.

"That's the way things were," said another neighbor. "I think it's kind of funny."

No one Osgood and I talked to was willing to let us use their names, which often happens when people are asked to talk about potentially incendiary topics.

"Let's just say it's not exactly politically correct," said another observer. "But I don't see the harm."

The ad was for Gold Dust Washing Powder, which was a popular cleaning product from the 1880s into the 1930s. It was originally made by the N. K. Fairbank Company, which also manufactured and sold such items as Santa Claus soap and a lard compound. The company was headed by Chicagoan Nathaniel Fairbank, who was known as the Lard King.

The Gold Dust Twins—their names were Dustie and Goldie, and some ads asked, "Are you a slave to housework?"—were probably second in "popularity" only to Aunt Jemima as black advertising characters. Take a trip on the Internet and you'll discover that items featuring the twins are highly prized by collectors of black memorabilia and race art. One site offers an unopened five-ounce box of Gold Dust for $124.

You can't see the sign on Irving Park. Joe Staszel, the man in Osgood's photo, and others have put up condos that cover the ad. But it makes you wonder what you might be in for the next time some building comes down in the name of progress. Will you get to glimpse a part of our past that's impossible not to look at but also painful to see?

AUGUST 31, 2003

NO ONE CAN REMEMBER seeing Richard J. Daley and Carl Sandburg together discussing the relative merits of smoked ham or sausages, but the mayor and the poet were both loyal customers of Drier's Meat Market, an ancient and thriving purveyor of smoked meats and cheeses in Three Oaks, Michigan, and likely the only meat market in the country to be listed in the National Register of Historic Places.

Drier's, originally a wagon repair shop, was taken over in 1875 by an Englishman named Alec Watson and transformed into the Union Meat Market. He hired ten-year-old Ed Drier as a delivery boy and later elevated the lad to the position of clerk. In 1913 Drier bought the store.

Drier's son, Ed Jr., ran the place for decades before his death in 1994. It was he who in the

AN ODE TO BOLOGNA

1960s decided not to compete with supermarkets in the fresh meat game and offered his own smoked hams, liver sausage, bratwurst, and the legendary bologna, which Drier always spelled "baloney." And it was he who gathered pals such as Daley, Sandburg, clothing designer Bill Blass, artists Ivan Albright and Bill Mauldin, actor Larry Hagman, and critic Roger Ebert, who lived or vacationed in the area.

Drier was an affable man, filled with lore and gossip that he was eager to share, often along with a shot from the bottle of Scotch he kept handy.

The store is now run by Ed Jr.'s daughter, Carolyn Drier, and her nephew, David Wooley, smiling in Osgood's photo.

The place is filled with many hats worn by the railroad men who once patronized the market. They and many other items make the store seem almost like a museum. And do buy some food. It's great, but don't take our word for it. Take the word of an anonymous poet doing his or her best Sandburg:

> Thank you, dear Eddie,
> For your bottles and basket.
> We've only one question
> And now we will ask it.
> We know cheese in a tub
> And liver's not bony.
> But how in the world
> Do you make your baloney?

SEPTEMBER 19, 2004

224

MR. BARBER

GETTING A SHAVE in a barbershop was already something of a novelty twenty-five years ago when a group of adventurous and fun-loving young reporters would go to the barbershop at the Drake Hotel and get shaves. We did this about once a month for a year, but on every visit we would find one of the chairs occupied by Judge Julius Hoffman of Chicago Seven trial infamy. We were told in a whisper that he was a daily shave customer, and he had what appeared to us to be a most difficult face for the straight razor, all jowly and frozen in what seemed like a perpetual frown.

There are still a few places in the area where you can pay a person to shave your face. The act is viewed by most as an exotic, indulgent experience, perhaps something you would buy as a gift for that proverbial man in your life.

"But they are a great experience," says Peter Vodovoz.

Vodovoz shaves people, perhaps ten a month (not including himself, doing the deed in Osgood's photo). He learned this craft in his native Russia, from which he emigrated in 1990. He arrived in Chicago with one dollar in his pocket, but thanks to some cousins who put him up and fed him, he was able to go to Truman College and learned to speak English, which led to a job cutting hair and giving shaves at the Drake Hotel barbershop.

In 2000 he opened his own shop (again, see Osgood's pic). It is tucked on the sixth floor of 67 East Oak Street. But it's a great place often filled with lively conversation.

It is certifiably barbershop rather than salon, a fact punctuated by its name, Mr. Barber on Oak, which is as marvelously straightforward as its slogan/claim: "We Make You Handsome."

Through word of mouth Vodovoz has built a long list of loyal clients, including some big names from the worlds of sports, business, and politics. Among the biggest is that of Illinois governor Rod Blagojevich.

"He's a super guy," says Vodovoz. "Yes, he has a lot of hair, but cutting it is easy and a lot of fun."

Vodovoz lives in the northern suburbs with his wife, Stella, and their daughter, Emily. His shop is open seven days a week. Asked what he and the governor talk about, Vodovoz says, "Many things, but I am always telling him, 'God bless America.'"

FEBRUARY 5, 2004

A DEADLY SHORTCUT

BOWMANVILLE AVENUE HUGS the southern edge of Rosehill Cemetery on the North Side, slicing diagonally through what appears to be a quiet and pleasant neighborhood. Driving down this street one afternoon, Osgood and I, much to our delight, saw some ducklings nosing around in the front yard of a house. But then, to our sorrow, we saw a small cross stuck in the ground near a tree. We knew immediately what it was. With as much driving around as we do, we often—too often—see roadside memorials. But we have found these to be more common in suburban or rural areas, where roads are wider and speed limits higher.

This cross had once been white but was faded to a sad shade of gray. A plastic rosary hung from it, and the cross had a name, Cady, and a date, December 14, 2002. At the center of the cross was a snapshot, a picture of a little girl and a dog. Both of them are sleeping.

That poor little girl, I thought, but I soon learned that it was not five-year-old Megan Andrews but her dog who was killed on a Saturday afternoon, a few feet from the intersection of Bowmanville and Bell Avenues. There is a stop sign at this corner, and therein lies one of the problems troubling neighborhood residents. In the windows of some homes are signs that read STOP THE BOWMANVILLE EXPRESSWAY.

"A normal city street like this gets about twelve hundred cars a day. We get nearly four thousand," says Betty Redmond, who has lived here for thirteen years. She has one of the signs in the window of her home. "We've been trying to fix this for the last seven years."

Bowmanville is the most convenient east-west street between Foster and Peterson Avenues in this area, and it is used as a shortcut between Damen and Western Avenues. Some people want speed bumps installed. Others want cops posted on the street. Something needs to be done. In the thirty or so minutes Osgood and I spent on Bowmanville, we watched dozens of cars zipping down the street at speeds far above the posted limit, many of them blowing through stop signs.

"I was almost sideswiped one morning while I was putting something in my car," says Redmond. "I feel a sense of danger whenever I'm out in the street."

Little Megan Andrews now has a new dog, and other neighborhoods have problems that might seem more serious than speeding cars: drugs, gangs, drive-bys, a lack of city services. But whether it concerns a child, an elderly person, or a dog named Cady, isn't it all about life and death?

JULY 13, 2003

228

AMERICAN DREAMER

WHEN HE ARRIVED IN CHICAGO in 1990 from his native Morocco, twenty-three-year-old Bouchaib Khribech was planning to stay with a friend of a friend. But when that person failed to show up to meet Khribech's plane at O'Hare, the young man spent his first days in town nervously sleeping on the El and camping out in Winnemac Park on Damen Avenue.

Ten days in town and he had himself a job busing tables at the Billy Goat Tavern. He's been there ever since, an ebullient presence, his English ever improving as he took the nickname Bouch, waited tables, tended bar, and grilled burgers.

"He is a good worker," says Sam Sianis, the Billy Goat's owner. "I am proud of him."

Bouch's bright smile and radiant personality have endeared him to the tavern's clientele. Many have become close friends. And he has been mentioned in many newspaper stories, especially when he became an American citizen in October 2000. This has not ruined Bouch. Neither has meeting former presidents Clinton and Bush and other "celebrities" who've dropped by for a burger and a photo opportunity. Bouch sent copies of the Christmas cards he got from the Clintons and the photo of himself and Bush I to the king of Morocco, who was so impressed that he invited Bouch's mom for a visit.

That mom, Zohra Chafki, is in Chicago now, as are his sister, Meryem, and two brothers, Marouane and Tarik. The entire family is involved in the launch of Bouch's new venture. It is called Marrakech ExpressO, at 4747 North Damen Avenue, and you'll be impressed by how Bouch and his family transformed the former Internet café into what is, as Bouch says, "the next best thing to visiting Morocco." It is a handsome space with a fourteen-hundred-square-foot main room and a larger area downstairs that Bouch hopes to use for private parties.

Bouch works seven days a week at the Billy Goat, always has, and plans to continue to do so. "It will be hard," he says, "but my family will help, and I like hard work."

The place will feature the familiar lineup of coffee drinks as well as smoothies and juices, cookies, pastries, and homemade goodies. "And from the start there will be soup and sandwiches and other dishes," says Bouch. "I want to compete with Starbucks. It is like a dream. When I first come here, I sleep in the park four blocks away. Now I have this. It will be hard, but I know I can do it. I know life is about challenge."

JULY 25, 2005

A COP WHO LOVED MUSIC

TUESDAY NIGHTS AT Chief O'Neill's Pub and Restaurant feature traditional Irish music and often include the pipe playing of Brendan McKinney, who opened this place at 3471 North Elston Avenue in 1999.

For reasons we don't want to explore, Osgood and I are often asked, "What makes a great Chicago saloon?" It's a hard question. We most often answer, "You'll know one when you're in one."

Many experts have weighed in on this matter. *New Yorker* writer A. J. Liebling observed in the 1950s: "A thing about Chicago that impressed me from the hour I got there was the saloon. New York bars operate on the principle that you want a drink or you wouldn't be there . . . Chicago bars assume that nobody likes liquor, and that to induce the customers to purchase even a minute quantity, they have to provide a show."

A few decades later, Mike Royko wrote, "[The new generation of young people] demanded more than the traditional neighborhood joints provided. They wanted entertainment, rock music, folk music, disco dancing, ski parties, dartboards . . . And, of course, they wanted to meet each other, which is where the Pill comes in. As much as anything, Chicago night life owes its explosive growth to ancient lusts now unshackled by science."

I didn't know Liebling, but I knew Royko and think he would have loved O'Neill's, not only for its lively barroom (we understand the restaurant serves good food) but also because the owners have a sense of history. They named the place in honor of Francis O'Neill, who in 1901 became Chicago's chief of police, presiding over a force of thirty-three hundred officers, of whom two thousand were Irish. After retiring in 1905, O'Neill put together the largest collection of Irish music ever printed.

A music-loving cop—right up Royko's alley. Too bad he's not here to enjoy the pleasures of this great saloon.

AUGUST 3, 2003

LOOK HOW HAPPY SHE IS, seventy-nine-year-old Anne Romagnoli. A life in music will do that to a person, even if that music is made by the often-derided accordion.

The model she is holding in Osgood's photo is one made in 1929 by the company her father and his brothers started in the early 1900s on Taylor Street. Demo Piatanesi and brothers Finau and Bramante later joined other craftsmen to form the Italo-American Accordion Company. It was headquartered at Fifty-first Street and Kedzie Avenue, where, at the height of the accordion's popularity in the late 1930s, a hundred workers were turning out more than twenty-five accordions a week.

In 1948 a man named Joe Romagnoli came to the United States as a sales representative for an Italian accordion company. He was in a real sense born to the business, having been raised

A BIG HUG

in Castelfidardo, where the first Italian accordion factory opened in 1863 and which would eventually become the center of accordion making. He and Anne fell in love and were married in 1948. He went to work for Italo-American and eventually took over the business.

In the 1950s the accordion was still in fashion, and a seven-year-old boy named Dennis DeYoung began seven years of accordion lessons. He quit music altogether at fourteen. But a year or two later he was walking down the streets of his Roseland neighborhood on the South Side and heard the Panozzo brothers, Chuck on guitar and John on drums, playing music with another kid on accordion. DeYoung soon replaced the accordion player and later switched to piano, and these three teenagers formed the nucleus of what would become the band Styx.

Not many former accordion players did as well (John Lennon did a little better), but many famous people played the accordion, including politicos Richard Nixon and H. Ross Perot, actors James Stewart and Charlie Chaplin, novelists Charles Dickens and Thomas Hardy, and Mahatma Gandhi. But the accordion business was not a good business. After Romagnoli took over the company in the early 1950s, there began a steady sales decline. Kids wanted to play guitars.

Until his death in 1994 at seventy-one, Romagnoli was arguably the last person in the United States who could create an accordion from scratch. Accordions are no longer made at the Italo-American Accordion Company, at 5510 West Ninety-fifth Street in Oak Lawn, but they sell and repair the instruments, and on occasion Anne Romagnoli can be persuaded to play a tune.

"When you play the accordion, it is very much like embracing someone," she says.

SEPTEMBER 18, 2005

THE LAST BEACH

CHICAGO'S SHORELINE STRETCHES thirty miles north from Indiana, ending at a tiny beach at its northern edge. Very few people, except some joggers, bicyclists, and those who live on the street closest to the beach, know of this slice of sand. It is not visible to the motorists who cruise by on nearby Sheridan Road as it twists into an S shape at the border of Evanston. North Eastlake Terrace is the name of the street, and it is one of the city's least known, running one way south off briefly-east-west Sheridan for only a few blocks.

Jane Flynn Royko is a marketing executive and actress who lived on North Eastlake from 1990 to 1997. No relation to the famous Chicago newspaper columnist, Royko now lives in Beverly with her husband, Mark, and their three-year-old son, Charlie.

"I miss the beach," she says. "I really loved it. It was such a secret little place, a little pearl. To be able to live on the lake and afford it."

The beach is bookended by piles of rocks that appear randomly arranged by years of beating waves. A dozen or so trees sprout defiantly from the northern rocks. In the soft seasons, the beach seems as if it has been stolen from California's Big Sur.

"I loved it most in the winter," says Royko. "The water would freeze and transform the beach and trees into these stunning ice sculptures."

The last building on the lake is a substantial four-story structure that makes a person instantly envious of the people who live there, some with decks that jut above the water. While exploring the beach, Osgood and I encountered a woman who said that she was the owner of that building. "My family has owned it since 1949," said Mrs. Jeffery Mattozzi. "It is not for sale. You can't buy it!"

Figures. Some people know when they've got a good thing.

JANUARY 23, 2000

ON THE ROAD TO NOWHERE

TIOGA TRAIL IS A STREET you have never heard of unless you live near the town of Rolling Prairie, Indiana, itself a place you probably never heard of unless you live nearby.

This is the time of year when many Chicago-area folks scoot up to their summer homes in Michigan, rarely venturing off the familiar route through Indiana and thus never walking into the bar/restaurant at 5868 East Tioga Trail, where they might hear the telephone ring and bartender Jeni Strieter answer, "Nowhere."

That's what it is: the Nowhere Bar and Grill. On the wall is an old menu from 1958, when the place was called the Saugany Lake Tavern and Restaurant and a T-bone went for $2.50. "I remember that," says Marv Williams, a retired carpenter who has been visiting Nowhere "damn near every day" since 1947, when he was served his first beer at age thirteen. He is sitting at the bar between two pals—Nowhere regulars Butch Siford (to his right in Osgood's picture) and Dale Bratton. That's Strieter behind the bar, and the guys call her "our sweetheart."

She's been working at Nowhere for three years, since Ted and Helen Pfauth bought it. Even they don't know how old the place is. "Our best guess is that it opened in the 1920s or even before. But we do know this building was moved up here, by the use of logs and horses, from the shore of Saugany Lake two blocks away in about 1946."

Nowhere is, in every way, a charming place, from the friendly crowd to the colorful decor, from the low prices to the food. (There's also a signed photo of Oprah Winfrey on the wall. Ask one of the regulars why.) The Pfauths expanded the menu and created the slogan "The Best Prime Rib Around," though Osgood was partial to the burgers and homemade desserts. Neither of us was bold enough to try the deep-fried black olives stuffed with salsa and cheese.

It would be impossible to give you directions to the place. Most people just stumble upon it. "That's how we first discovered it," says Ted Pfauth.

So the best thing to do is call for directions. You may still get lost making your way there, but once you arrive, you'll be onto a wonderful secret: Nowhere is really something.

MAY 18, 2003

NEW VOICES IN THE PARK

IT IS, LIKE ALL PARKS, a place of shadow and light, and late on this lazy summer afternoon the small green square of the city is a shared space. To three kids on the edge of their teens, this is Li'l Park, a place with enough concrete at its center to allow for in-line skating. To others, spread across benches and grass with their meager belongings piled nearby, it is Newberry Park, for the dark brick library that faces it on the north.

Its formal name is Washington Square Park, but to most it is Bughouse Square, and it is a slice of Chicago that symbolizes freedom of assembly and expression.

Chicago's oldest public park, it was deeded to the city more than 150 years ago and immediately became a gathering place for those who felt the urge to stand on soapboxes and speak their minds. Some were famous: Carl Sandburg, Emma Goldman. Others were anonymous anarchists, dreamers, poets, preachers, and nuts.

Today, whatever echoes exist of dead debates are overwhelmed by the laughter of three kids, the skid of skates. These are summer days filled with play, futures filled with light. "What do you want to be when you grow up?" they are asked, and answers arrive with the force of assurance that can come from kids soon to enter seventh grade at a prestigious private school: "Entrepreneur." "Lawyer." "Paparazzi." The kids have heard that a fence is to be built around the park. Some adults decry the fence. Studs Terkel has said, "A fence would be a desecration. What is a fence? Something to keep people out."

The kids don't care. "It'll be nicer," says one.

James Walker agrees. He is sitting alone, only a few feet from the kids but a world apart: neighbor and stranger.

"I come here a lot," he says. "It is peaceful. I sit here. I sit here because . . ."

The words roll off his tongue at a gentle pace and then stop. He is forty-six years old but looks decades older. He is from Chicago and is unemployed, though he used to work. "In a hospital," he says, with pride. "In housekeeping."

"A fence?" he says. "That's okay."

It is hot, very hot, and in time Walker leaves the bench and walks to a patch of grass. He lies down in the shade and smokes the one cigarette he has, given to him by a stranger. The kids skate in the sunlight, not yet ready to go home.

AUGUST 9, 1998

240

ACKNOWLEDGMENTS

We would like to thank the *Chicago Tribune,* which not only provides us a place to work but also allows us to collaborate with relatively little interference. *Chicago Tribune Magazine* editor Elizabeth Taylor deserves credit for allowing *Sidewalks* to be born. Jeff Lyon, Marshall Froker, Brenda Butler, Nancy Watkins, Margaret Carroll, Jean Rudolph, Barb Sutton, and Desiree Chen exercised their expert editorial skills to make each column better than it was when I wrote it. Associate managing editor of photography Torry Bruno has been steady in his support of Osgood's efforts, and magazine photo editor Mike Zajakowski has always made Osgood sweat in the cause of better pictures. David Syrek and Joe Darrow have made the magazine sparkle with their attention to detail and design. Without Anna Seeto's organizational skills, the magazine would never make it into the Sunday paper, and she is always on the lookout for *Sidewalks* subjects. Randy Weissman, deputy managing editor, gently guided us along the newspaper-to-book road. Susan Betz, the editor in chief of Northwestern University Press, came up with the idea of this book and has been its champion. She also put us into the capable and artful hands of Amy Schroeder, Nora Gorman, Laura Leichum, Parneshia Jones, Kim Bartko, and Marianne Jankowski; they are a dream team. There are others: Richard Christiansen for his ongoing enthusiasm and inspiration, not merely for this project but throughout our careers; David Phillips for his brilliant eye and counsel; photo department colleagues Todd Panagopoulos, Frank Hanes, and Jennifer Fletcher for invaluable aid and counsel; and Kemper Kirkpatrick for his sleuthing skills. Our families and friends—you know who you are and we feel fortunate that there are too many of you to mention here—keep us as happy as we are capable of being. Finally, we are most deeply indebted to the people we have met in this ongoing adventure that is *Sidewalks,* grateful that they allowed us into their lives and let us tell their stories.

CHRIS WALKER

ABOUT THE AUTHORS

Born and raised in Chicago, RICK KOGAN began his newspaper career at sixteen. He has worked for the *Chicago Daily News, Chicago Sun-Times,* and *Chicago Tribune,* where he is a senior writer and columnist for the Sunday magazine. He is the author of ten books, including *Yesterday's Chicago* (in collaboration with his father, journalist and historian Herman Kogan); *Everybody Pays: Two Men, One Murder, and the Price of Truth* (with Maurice Possley); *America's Mom: The Life, Lessons, and Legacy of Ann Landers;* and *A Chicago Tavern: A Goat, a Curse, and the American Dream.* He is also the creator and host of WGN's *Sunday Papers with Rick Kogan.*

CHARLES OSGOOD was born in Milwaukee and raised in Wauwatosa, Wisconsin. He attended Ripon College and received a master of fine arts in photography from the School of the Art Institute of Chicago. After beginning his career at the City News Bureau, he came to the *Chicago Tribune* as a reporter, switching to photography, his lifelong passion, in 1970. Since then assignments have taken him along sidewalks around the world.